Lilies

The Royal Horticultural Society

Michael Jefferson-Brown

Special photography
Andrew Lawson

Lilies

A guide to choosing and
growing lilies

Quadrille

Publishing Director Jane O'Shea
Art Director Helen Lewis
Project Editor Carole McGlynn
Art Editor Paul Welti
Photography Andrew Lawson, Sarah Cuttle
Production Beverley Richardson, Vincent Smith

First published in 2003 by Quadrille Publishing Limited

Cataloguing-in-Publication Data: a catalogue record for this book
is available from the British Library.

ISBN   1-84400-035-4
Printed and bound in China

Half-title (page 1): Oriental hybrid lily of the Orienpet
Group, *Lilium* 'Black Beauty'

Title (pages 2–3): Candidum Group species lily,
Lilium pyrenaicum

This page: Asiatic hybrid lily, *Lilium* 'Lollipop'

Opposite page: Oriental hybrid lily of the Orienpet
Group, *Lilium* 'Catherine the Great'

contents

I admit to an infatuation with all lilies –
I find them both intriguing and exciting. Their
diversity in appearance is allied to a many-
faceted worth in the garden that makes them
an increasingly important ornamental plant.

introducing lilies

Lilies of one kind or another look set to make
the most of the opportunities offered by the
size and form of today's gardens and, with
their drought resistance, to exploit our
apparently changing climate patterns. We shall
be looking at the species to suggest the most
suitable for a variety of sites, while the legion
of hybrids will test our discrimination.

Lilies have always been regarded as something special, as glamorous plants. They have been associated with mankind for millennia, being used both decoratively and as a source of food and of medicine. Some, such as the Madonna lily (*L. candidum*), were used in religious observances in times well before the Christian era.

introducing lilies: history

The Madonna lily (*L. candidum*) has been grown in Europe as a fodder and decorative plant for at least 2,500 years, especially around the Mediterranean. Today it is as much a favourite of modest cottage gardens as of stately homes.

Once the showy flowers of wild lilies caught the eye of plant hunters, bulbs were collected and sent from their native habitats to those parts of the world where gardens were established. By the sixteenth century there were already several species in cultivation in Europe. The introduction of new species gained momentum as China and the Far East were more fully explored during the second half of the nineteenth century and the beginning of the twentieth. A number of naturally occurring hybrids had been found in the wild and more arose under cultivation, but it was not until halfway through the twentieth century that the real hybrid revolution got under way.

These are exciting times for lilies. The new hybrids being bred are often kinds only dreamt of a few decades ago. The huge size of some of the newer Oriental hybrids may cause some slight unease but the other fields of breeding activity can be wholeheartedly welcomed. The Asiatics will retain their appeal, but the result of mating these with *L. longiflorum* has produced a hugely robust race of large, showy, garden-worthy stars. In another direction, the influence of the lime-tolerant *L. henryi* in the cross-breeding of Orientals may be the most important long-term advance for gardeners, producing plants that can be grown in soils of widely different pH values but with the opulent beauty of the lime-hating Orientals.

earliest times

The illustrations are taken from John Parkinson's *Paradisi in Sole Paradisus Terrestris* of 1629, 'The Garden of Pleasant Flowers'. The flowers from left to right are as then listed, with their present-day names in brackets.
1 Martagon Flore albo. The white Martagon (*L. martagon* var. *album*).
2 Martagon five. Lilium canadense maculatum. The spotted Martagon or Lily of Canada (*L. canadense*).
3 Martagon Pomponeum. The Martagon Pompony or early red Martagon (*L. pomponium*).

It is impossible to pinpoint the first time that human culture became closely associated with lilies and to be sure which was the first species so favoured, but the joint favourites are the tiger lily (*L. lancifolium*) and the Madonna lily (*L. candidum*). The tiger lily has formed a part of the staple diet in regions of China for thousands of years, where it would appear that various forms have been selected to grow as a fodder crop; perhaps the fairly widespread distribution of the triploid form (having three sets of chromosomes) may be put down to its usefulness and vigour. The native peoples of North America also used many bulbs, including lilies, as food, a practice that presumably stretched back into the mists of antiquity.

The claims for the Madonna lily to be the first one intimately associated with mankind again rest primarily on its use as food, but the flowers were widely linked with religious and civic ceremonial. This lily appears as a decorative motif in a Minoan fresco found at Amnissos, near Knossos on the Greek island of Crete, now housed in the Heraklion Museum. Just when the fresco was made is uncertain but the Minoan civilization dates as far back as 3000–1500BC. Representations of the Madonna lily can also be found in the work of the Assyrians and the early Egyptians. Only later did it become associated with Christianity, as one of many plants grown by monks for their medicinal properties, real or imagined. It was known as a symbol for St John the Baptist and for a series of other saints and was first firmly linked with the Virgin Mary in 1043 in Spain, where the bulbs may have been introduced by the Moors. But it is with the Renaissance that *L. candidum* became the unequivocal symbol for the Mother of Christ – the Madonna lily.

From early on, bulbs of *L. candidum* were spread all over the countries around the Mediterranean and further afield; the Phoenicians as the great sailor-traders of early times have been given credit for much of this dispersal. The original home of the species is now assumed to have been the eastern Mediterranean and the Balkans. Happily the species proved an amenable one and by the beginning of the nineteenth century it had become a familiar plant in cottage gardens as well as in those of the large estates. Its success as a cottage garden plant was probably due to being allowed its own undisturbed regime, growing away from other lilies. Its vulnerability to virus diseases has been such that stocks have been weakened and eventually killed when attacked by viruses that have had less effect on other species.

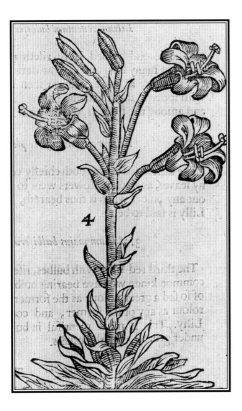

4 Lilium album. The white lily
(*L. candidum*)

INTO GARDENS: EUROPEAN SPECIES

Collections of diverse plants were built up in scholastic and monastic centres, often for their possible medicinal value. Herbals show that several European species were being grown in both institutional and private gardens as early as 1597. The herbal of the botanist John Gerard dating from this time lists five kinds – *L. candidum, L. bulbiferum, L. croceum, L. chalcedonicum* and *L. martagon*. John Parkinson in his *Paradisi in Sole Paradisus Terrestris* of 1629 adds three new kinds – *L. pyrenaicum* and *L. pomponium*, both from European mountain ranges, as well as *L. canadense*, an early entry from North America.

Of these species it is the martagon lily that is now the most popular. Earlier herbals showed *L. martagon* to be well established as a garden plant since the fifteenth century. Though it is doubtful whether any medicinal role was found for this lily, its decorative value must have been recognized, since bulbs were spread around all the main European gardens. The martagons are much prized for their longevity, their graceful long spires of nodding flowers and a pleasing colour range from pure white through pinks to some dark maroon-red forms such as *L. martagon* var. *cattaniae*.

The European *L. bulbiferum*, with wide open bowls of orange or rich gold, is the species that has joined with a clutch of lilies from the Far East to produce the hugely successful Asiatic hybrids. It is an exuberant, fast-growing, very early-flowering plant, but in cultivation is best moved and propagated frequently as it can exhaust a location and die out. Another long-cultivated European, *L. pyrenaicum*, usually the first lily to bloom, is distinctly different. Formerly more widespread in gardens than it is at present, it has bulbs of many narrow scales, lots of narrow, bright green foliage clustered around the stems and plenty of nodding, dark-spotted turk's cap flowers, usually coloured deep lemon.

AMERICAN AND ASIATIC SPECIES

The people that settled in America discovered there a new flora. Lilies were sent back into Europe but only a few became established garden plants. The most robust proved to be *L. pardalinum*, a useful species that can be planted and left for many years. One of the most prized finds was *L. canadense* and this remains a favourite of lily fanciers but, despite its early introduction into Europe by 1629, the secret of growing it well has yet to be uncovered. It can flourish in some gardens and fail in the one next door, or it can do well for several years and then decline. Its relatively large flowers in gold or orange are gracefully held, hanging but with its pointed petals swept in a graceful arc.

The exploration of the East, especially China, was often led by missionaries, many of whom were fascinated by the botanical wildlife of the country and would

L. lancifolium var. splendens is a strong form of an exuberant species that has long been a favourite garden plant and is one of the most important founder species of the Asiatic hybrids.

make collections. Père David was one and his name is commemorated in the species *L. davidii*, an attractive lily with orange pendent blooms. In gardens it has been somewhat in the shadow of the tiger lily (*L. lancifolium*, formerly *L. tigrinum*), which took to cultivation very easily. This was hardly surprising as it had been widely grown for centuries as a food plant.

The long-term isolation of Japan from international trade and communication meant that it was difficult to obtain plants indigenous to that country, of which there were several lily species and some hybrids tended by gardeners there. Two kinds were outstanding, distinct from all others and perhaps encapsulating some of the mystery of the East: *L. speciosum* and *L. auratum*. The first has stalked leaves and recurving, nodding flowers in white and pink, all held in airy heads within a cloud of perfume, while the second has large flowers with wide petals and a voluptuous scent. It was flowered in Britain in 1862 and shown at the Royal Horticultural Society in July of that year, where it created a horticultural sensation (see page 14).

Lilium auratum was first shown by the famous Veitch nursery, one of the most active in the nineteenth and twentieth centuries, which arranged for the introduction of many plants from Asia. A major importation of *L. auratum* took place from 1877 to 1879 and it is thought that the numbers being sent to Europe in later years reached into millions. This was not an unqualified success, however, as bulbs were susceptible to basal rot in transit and became prey to virus in European gardens. They fared better in warmer climates, such as Oregon and parts of New Zealand. Nowadays it is the hybrid series from the cross-breeding of *L. auratum* and *L. speciosum* that play a major role in the garden and these have proved much easier to grow.

China seemed to be an inexhaustible treasure store of all types of lilies, particularly Trumpets, though not all grew with unrestrained vitality in gardens. Most are beautiful white flowers: *L. leucanthum*, *L. longiflorum* and *L. wallichianum* were plants of the mainland, while *L. philippinense* and *L. formosanum* were named after their island homes. Commercially, *L. longiflorum*, the Easter lily, was by far the most important. It was easy to propagate from seed and the blooms have for a century been prized as cut flowers; they are grown under glass in Europe and many other countries but will succeed in the open in milder climates. The two yellow-flowered species, *L. sargentiae* and *L. sulphureum*, have proved trickier to keep healthy in gardens but have made a valuable contribution to the breeding of strong golden hybrids. None of these species, however, has had such an impact on the gardening scene in Europe, North America, the Antipodes and elsewhere as *L. regale*.

THE REGAL LILY STORY

At the turn of the nineteenth century the young Ernest Wilson was engaged by the Veitch nursery to go to China to seek seeds of the handkerchief tree (*Davidia involucrata*) and others. In 1903 he found himself in the Min valley of western Szechwan, a narrow gorge with high, precipitous sides. It happened that a particular lily was in bloom, with thousands of stems leaning from the sides and spilling their perfume on the air. He had discovered the only known habitat of *L. regale*, which some would regard as the most splendid and successful of lilies in our gardens. He described what may have been the most exciting moment in the history of plant hunting:

L. regale was blessed by a robust constitution: the bulbs grew well under cultivation and freely produced seed that developed rapidly into flowering plants.

'There, in narrow, semi-arid valleys down which thunder torrents, and encompassed by mountains composed of mudshales and granites, whose peaks are clothed with snow eternal, the Regal Lily has its home. In summer the heat is terrific, in winter the cold is intense, and at all seasons these valleys are subject to sudden and violent windstorms against which neither man nor beast can make headway. There, in June, by the wayside, in rock crevices by the torrent's edge, and high up on the mountainside and precipice, this lily in full bloom greets the weary wayfarer. Not in twos or threes but in hundreds, in thousands, aye, in tens of thousands. Its slender stems, each from two to four feet tall, flexible and tense as steel, overtopping the coarse grass and scrub, are crowned with one to several large funnel-shaped flowers more or less wine-coloured without, pure white and lustrous on the face, clear canary-yellow within the tube and each stamen filament tipped with a golden anther. The air in the cool of the morning and in the evening is laden with delicious perfume exhaled from each bloom. For a brief season this lonely, semi-desert is transformed by this Lily into a veritable fairy-land.'

Wilson harvested many bulbs and introduced them into Europe and America. A consignment of around 3,000 was sent back to Veitch's nursery in the autumn of 1904. It bloomed for the first time in Britain the following year and has featured in the lists of all the main bulb dealers ever since.

how lilies were first grown

L. auratum caused a sensation when it was introduced into Europe from Japan in the 1860s. With the largest flowers of the genus, perhaps as much as 25–30cm (10–12in) across, it was one of the wonders of the natural world. The wide open flowers vary in size and in colour around a standard white with a star of gold formed by the central stripe down each petal that gave it its common name, golden-ray lily.

Through the nineteenth and early twentieth centuries new importations of bulbs from the East were eagerly sought. Many of the newly discovered lilies were the playthings of the wealthy and a source of rivalry between the owners of stately homes. The Trumpets were much prized but probably the most sought after were the *L. auratum* forms. Growers vied with each other to produce the largest flowers and the most massive heads of bloom. In the 1869 September issue of *The Floral World* is a report which is a eulogy to the species and gives a flavour both of the social mores of the time and of the genteel competitive spirit among the aristocracy.

'*Lilium auratum* is only just beginning to show its true capabilities. Messrs. Standish and Co. of Ascot have had a plant in bloom during the past month, with a single stem measuring 13 feet in height, and bearing upwards of a hundred flowers. At a committee meeting of the Royal Horticultural Society, on the 17th ult., Mr Goode, gardener to the Dowager Lady Ashburnam, Melchet Court, Romney, Hants, exhibited a grand specimen, with the main stems nine feet high, measuring 1 inch in diameter at a foot from the surface of the soil, besides smaller stems, bearing altogether 152 flowers – a wonderful example of cultural skill.'

Gardeners were inclined almost to force-feed their plants, a regime that usually ended in disaster as the bulbs were unaccustomed to such rich fare. In their wild homes the species was used to the meagre diet of the ash soil of quiescent Japanese volcanoes. Cultivators in Europe at the end of the growing season might turn out their pots to find that the bulb had disappeared. There had been no hint of trouble above ground; the stem and flower had been fed and supported by the extensive roots from the stem, an instance of how effective and important this annually renewed stem-rooting can be.

E. H. Wilson writes of seeing the species growing wild:

'In Japan there is much poor and hungry soil but none more so than the slopes of august Fiji and the volcanic deposits of the neighbouring Idzu province. Around Matsushima, a beauty spot in northern Japan, I saw this Lily in quantity growing in coarse grey sandstone rock. In western Japan, in the province of Uzen, I also met

L. martagon **var.** *cattaniae* **'The Moor'** is a selected clone from the dark-flowered form of the species familiar in European gardens for over five centuries.

with it growing wild on gravelly banks and hillsides amongst small shrubs and coarse grasses. It is the open, porous soil, and not the rich humus, that this Lily luxuriates in. Leafsoil it loves, in common with all Lilies, but it wants no unaerated acid peat and it loathes raw nitrogenous manures.'

I have kept the capital L used by Wilson for the word lily – I like the idea of our flower being so honoured.

Up to the time of the outbreak of the First World War, cottage gardens could boast of clumps of *L. candidum*, often one of the relatively few flowers growing among the vegetables. The species *L. martagon, L. bulbiferum* and *L. pyrenaicum* might also have been grown, a legacy of the monastery herbal gardens of the Middle Ages. In more sophisticated gardens much of the effort in lily culture for the 50 or so years before the outbreak of the Second World War was directed towards trying to arrange particular cultural conditions that the imported species would enjoy – an endeavour that tended to be rewarded rather intermittently.

THE ADVANCE OF MODERN HYBRIDS

The Japanese may have been the first to raise large numbers of lilies from seed, using their native species together with kinds introduced from China, of which *L. maculatum* and *L. dauricum* were the most significant. Growing together, cross-pollination occurred and a race of hybrid kinds was brought into Europe and marketed by the Dutch growers as *L. × maculatum*. Relatively easy plants to grow, these were the precursors of our modern Asiatic hybrids. During the 1930s and 1940s, the Dutchman Jan de Graaff gathered together as many species and cultivars as he could at his Oregon Bulb Farms and, with a dedicated team, started a huge cross-breeding programme (see page 74). Many of the Asiatics could trace some of their ancestry to the *L. × maculatum* series and to the Dutch-raised kinds bred from these with the European species *L. bulbiferum* – hybrid races known as *L. × hollandicum* and *L. × umbellatum*. Some of the resulting seedlings were introduced as Mid-Century Group. And since the middle of the last century most lily types have been successfully hybridized, some more extensively than others, which has given us a huge range of marvellous garden plants.

'Star Gazer' has proved the most successful of florist's lilies and is probably the most important cut flower of any kind ever cultivated.

Breeding now takes place in many countries throughout the world. Not only are modern hybrids easy to grow but they can be propagated without any special expertise, which means that commercially huge numbers can be grown rapidly. The cut-flower industry uses millions of bulbs where gardens are using thousands or tens of thousands; therefore much more work is done to produce cultivars that make good cut flowers. Upward-facing kinds are the easiest to cut and pack, so these dominate the market. Since the 1950s, the Asiatics have been the backbone of the flower trade but now the larger cultivars derived from hybridizing the Easter lily (*L. longiflorum*) with the Asiatics, commonly called LA hybrids, are taking over the florists as they grow easily and have larger flowers. They also have in their favour the ease with which flowers can be produced at any time of the year.

The Dutch flower market at Aalsmeer handles huge quantities of lilies that get exported all over the world, so that they have become a familiar part of every florist's display. In the year 2000 the prize for the greatest acreage of an individual cultivar was easily won by 'Star Gazer', with 225 hectares, while the white Oriental 'Siberia' came second with 186 hectares. The gardener also benefits from this intensive breeding. The LA hybrids are marvellous garden plants and the straightforward Asiatics are still available in a wide variety. Dwarf kinds, particularly suitable for pot culture, have established a strong niche in the market. The fantastic Oriental hybrids make choice cut flowers so they are being intensively bred, but gardeners with lime-free soils can make exotic pictures with these lilies in the open, while others use them as effectively as pot plants. And now we have a series of hybrids from the blending of Orientals with the blood line of *L. henryi*, giving a wonderful set of plants that inherit the lime-tolerance of the species.

what is a lily?

Lilies are normally very generous with their seed and *L. martagon*, shown here, could be the most profligate of all. Since each pod may contain 40–100 seeds, one can gauge the proportions of a possible population explosion.

The name lily has been used loosely for many hundreds of years, often to mean little more than 'flower' – possibly one with some resemblance to a true lily. A glance at the list of 'false' lilies (see page 160) will show that there are many of these and all but one are not even members of the large lily family, let alone of the *Lilium* genus. Perhaps we should give some specifications for a real lily.

The genus belongs to the northern hemisphere, with 80–100 species scattered through Europe, Asia and North America. They are all bulbous plants, though the form of the bulb varies considerably, and plant size ranges from a few centimetres high to over 3m (10ft) tall. Plants generally die down for the winter, with only *L. candidum* and one or two rare species maintaining a rosette of leaves through the winter to gain evergreen status.

The lily is a dynamo of energy, in a hurry to grow, bloom and increase. The seeds are flat discs that are piled up like plates in the seedpod – two piles in each of the three chambers – and it is not unusual to harvest over a hundred viable seeds from a pod. In the wild, as the ripe pod splits this seed will fall and be blown about to suitable and unsuitable nursery spots. Usually only a tiny proportion will germinate to grow to flowering-sized plants. Under controlled conditions, however, the gardener can often achieve an almost 100 per cent germination.

The seedlings of most lilies produce a single cotyledon leaf, strap-shaped and often carrying the seed case like a flag at its tip. Shortly after the first true leaf appears, elliptic or spear-shaped, tiny bulbs start to be formed. Some lily types miss out the cotyledon stage by forming embryo bulbs with roots by the side of the seed, only breaking through the soil surface with their first true leaves much later. Given suitable conditions, the small bulbs of most types grow quickly, doubling, quadrupling and further increasing their bulk in a matter of a few weeks. This process is accompanied by the production of more leaves until there is a mini-rosette of foliage. Stronger plants may try to produce a wiry stem with a complement of little leaves in the first growing season, but most will wait for their second year to do this and may or may not manage to top their stem with a bloom.

LILY BULBS

All the most popular lilies, such as the Asiatic hybrids, the Trumpets and the Orientals, have round, concentric bulbs made up of scales that are concave and wrap around the inner scales and growing centre. The scales can be narrow and tightly incurved, but are more usually wide enough to encircle a quarter, a third or even half of the bulb. The flowering stem arises though the middle, often called a 'nose'. After the growing season the stem dies down and, in doing so, will often divide the bulb into two. The two new growing points are clearly seen; depending on the age and vigour of the bulbs, the tissue joining the two potential new bulbs will begin to fail and twins result.

Some American species, including *L. pardalinum*, and their hybrids have a different lifestyle. The bulbs have scales but these are openly scattered along a rhizomatous rootstock, with only the growing points having newer, paler scales gathered together to show where the next flowering stems will emerge. The older scales and rootstock persist for a considerable time so that over the years an undisturbed bulb will form a wide mat of rootstock and scales. Gardeners impatient to propagate such bulbs will be forced to operate with a sharp knife, making sure that each severed portion has at least one growing point (see page 142). One or two species, such as *L. canadense*, appear to have ordinary concentric bulbs but by the end of the season each of these may have sent sideways one or more thick stolons, like reaching arms at the end of which new bulbs form.

A few Asian species, such as *L. duchartrei*, employ yet another method of bulb increase; they are known as stoloniferous-stemmed bulbs. The bulbs send up stems from what look like traditional concentric bulbs, but instead of making straight for the surface they wander around below, and at intervals along this wayward stem new bulbs form. The stem eventually breaks the surface and does the traditional lily performance. The gardener needs to be careful working around these plants as there is no telling where the underground stem and new bulbs might be. Sometimes the flowering stem can be 30–60cm (1–2ft) from its parent bulb. Unrelated lilies, both species and hybrids, may on occasion make a weak attempt to copy this behaviour. Certainly it is never wise to assume that a bulb is directly below the flowering stem – a warning that is best heeded when inserting canes or other supports after bulbs have been planted.

THE ROOTS

Roots emerge from the basal 'plate' of the bulb, to which the scales are affixed. These roots are of two types. There are fat, strong ones clearly marked with a series of rings and these plunge deep in the ground and are able to contract, concertina-wise, to pull bulbs lower down into the soil. This is a valuable operation, particularly with stem bulbils that fall to the ground and need to make their way deeper down to establish themselves. The more numerous roots are the fibrous ones that, with their multitude of root hairs, make intimate contact with the soil and feed the plant from the nutrient-laden soil water.

Many lilies also develop roots from the stem between the bulb and the soil surface. In some these are a token feature but in most they form an extensive

1 Concentric bulbs Most lily bulbs are concentric; they vary in size and depth but are basically formed of concave scales, tightly arranged around the central growing point. Some narrow scales are looser.

2 Concentric bulbs with waisted scales Bulbs of the *L. martagon* group have waisted scales that are easily fractured at this narrower point.

3 Rhizomatous bulbs A number of American species have these unusual bulbs. The scales are so brittle that, if roughly handled, a shower of scales is broken away. Each scale has the potential to become a new plant but a badly depleted bulb will be somewhat weakened until it gets re-established.

4 Stoloniferous bulbs These bulbs of *L. canadense* show how a parent bulb sends out strong stolons to the side, with new bulbs forming at the end of each. This method of bulbous increase is used by only a few species, but where one of these feels happy it will ensure that a good stand is quickly established.

network that undertakes two jobs – the effective augmentation of the feeding system and an anchor for the stem. The stem bearing flowers could easily be rocked to and fro without the support offered by the rooted part of the stem. These stem roots are not usually equally distributed along the stem but appear as so many rings, with lesser numbers between.

LILY FOLIAGE

Lily leaves are normally elliptic, but they vary in width, colour and method of display. It is supposed that the evolutionary prototype lily had leaves arranged in whorls, as in those of the present-day *L. martagon* and *L. pardalinum*. However, the more usual fashion is to have leaves scattered up the stem, sometimes with an incipient spiral pattern discernible. Some lilies have a wealth of leaves, others are sparingly endowed. They may be clasped tightly to the stem but examples can be found at every intermediate stage through to those held at right angles to the stem or even arching downwards. Normally they are joined directly to the stem but

SOME FORMS OF LILY FOLIAGE

Whorled foliage Members of the Martagon Group and a considerable number of North American species have their foliage arranged in formal whorls. The lower whorls are larger than those above, and towards the top of the stem there may be individual leaflets.

Scattered foliage This is the most usual form of lily foliage. Trumpet lilies often have tall stems with lots of very narrow leaves, sometimes darkly coloured, while Asiatic hybrids usually have fleshier, broader leaves that are bright green, though in some the foliage may be suffused with some darker colouring.

***Lilium speciosum* foliage** Several of the Oriental species have some or all of their leaves held by distinct leaf stems. The leaves are often arranged alternately up the stem and are more spear-shaped than many. They can give a 'classier' feel to the assemblage.

L. lancifolium var. flaviforum, showing dark bulbils in the leaf axils, a characteristic of all forms of the species.

some Eastern species, the Orientals and their hybrid derivatives, may have leaf stalks that give a distinct appearance and a more airy manner. Leaf colour ranges from pale green to a darkened purple that can be almost black.

LILY STEMS

The speed with which lilies grow in the spring is exciting. Once they have broken through the surface one can almost stand and watch them rocket upwards. The stems of most are as strong and erect as bamboos; indeed, the dead stems can often be used as temporary canes. Many species grow wild in scrubland and here the arching stems of a few kinds may lean on their neighbours for extra support. Stem colour may be an unblemished green but this is often suffused with a dark purple-maroon that can be so intense as to make them appear black, as in *L. lancifolium* or 'Festival'. Dark stems may or may not be matched to deep-toned foliage and dark flowers.

The obvious job of the stems is to support foliage and flowers and this may not be a light task, since a payload of 50–100 sizeable flowers is possible. The stems may have another function. Many lily types will produce bulblets on the length of stem below ground, these varying from tiny embryo ones to others as large as marbles or golf balls. A lesser number of lilies will mimic the behaviour of the tiger lily (*L. lancifolium*) by manufacturing large quantities of dark bulbils in the leaf axils. Sometimes more than one is grown in the leaf axil and, as there are plenty of leaves, a stem may give birth to a hundred or so bulbils. There is competition to be the mother of the year.

The late-flowering *L. speciosum* is outward- or downward-facing and is one of the most elegant of all lilies.

LILY FLOWERS

We move from the working parts to the main glory of the plant. Few can fail to be impressed by the floral displays of a lily, which can range from one or two flowers only a few centimetres high (as in *L. formosanum* var. *pricei* or some of the species from Tibet), to the towering heads of dozens of flowers held up to 3m (10ft) aloft. The number of blooms can border on the ridiculously prolific; I remember as a six-year-old helping my father to count a total of over 150 flowers on a stem of *L. davidii* var. *willmottiae*. A similar count is possible on a well-grown, well-established bulb of 'Black Beauty'.

The colour palette is wide, from white (sometimes greenish) to deepest yellow, and from orange through to red. A new Antipodean lily is described as 'black'. The permutations of colour combination are huge, sometimes one colour merging with or overlaying another. Contrasting shades or colours can be applied as beauty spots, veining, picotee work (pale, edged with a darker colour) or laid on as brushstrokes.

The pose of flowers is important and here the cut-flower market has exerted a huge influence on breeding. The need for easily cut and packed flowers has meant that upward-facing cultivars exceed outward-facing and pendent kinds by a ratio far in excess of a hundred to one. This turns on its head the usual dress mode of wild lilies, which favour a pendent or semi-pendent pose, the better to protect their pollen supplies and the receptive stigmas. There are nevertheless important species, such as *L. bulbiferum* and *L. dauricum*, that rebel and blatantly display sky-staring flowers seeking to attract passing insects to help with pollination.

While the gardener sees the flower as one having six petals, the botanist sees an outer ring of three sepals and an inner ring of three petals; if he deigns to amalgamate them, he maintains his professional dignity by terming them 'tepals'. We shall be happy with 'petals'. These may be more or less even-textured, but will have nectary channels leading towards the centre for the convenience of insects. The nectary channels may be differently coloured, perhaps green, to paint a central six-pointed star. Some kinds have a number of raised pimples on the inner surfaces, eruptions that are more correctly termed papillae. *L. henryi* curls back

The pendent *L. henryi* makes a feature of its papillae, a pattern of eruptions that are completely natural and call for no medical diagnosis. Other species have similar features, though usually less numerous, but sometimes made conspicuous by being flecked with an alternative petal colour.

its petals to display numerous large papillae and *L. speciosum* and Oriental hybrids are usually fairly well endowed, the papillae often being made more noticeable by having their tips touched with colour.

While the normal complement is of six petals, there are cultivars in which the sexual parts – stamens and stigma – have been transmuted into petaloids to give double flowers. In some, such as the Asiatic 'Fata Morgana', the extra petals are somewhat smaller and more or less overlay the original six; the doubling is certainly not excessive and could be overlooked at a distance. 'Pamela Jean' is a lightly doubled orange LA hybrid and there is a series marketed as Kiss Lilies that are dwarf Asiatics without pollen, most of which have the traditional six petals but some tend to produce a number of extra smaller petals.

There are now a number of more formidable doubles, flowers that look clearly distinct from traditional types. An Australian lily, 'Miss Lucy', is a starry white flower with just a whisper of green and pink which has up to 18 petals, the extra ones initially gathered together to form a projecting nose from the centre of each bloom. An American lily bred by the specialist Judith Freeman outdoes all other doubles. It is an Oriental called 'Flying Circus' with up to 50 petals! There are so many that the flower reaches forward, with six or seven layers of pointed petals. Opening in shades of pale green, the blooms end up pure white as the flower opens, reaches out and matures over a period of weeks through mid- to late summer. It will certainly shock the purist.

The form of the flower can be described as trumpet, bowl-shaped, starry, recurving or as 'turk's cap'. This last is really an outdated reference to the suggested similarity in appearance to the Turkish headwear abolished early in the twentieth century and now usually only met with in the pantomime character Aladdin. The usefulness of the term seems sure to ensure its survival to describe the rolled-back form of flowers such as those of *L. martagon* or *L. lancifolium*.

'Snow Star' clearly displays the upward-facing pose of the vast majority of Asiatic hybrids.

We now move into the garden and are ready to deploy our bulbs. Lilies can lay claim to being the ideal plants for the twenty-first-century garden, as they grow rapidly, they enjoy the company of shrubs and other plants, and die down quite discreetly. Potted bulbs on the point of bloom can be brought forward to enliven the patio or any other part of the garden and can be dropped into a border,

introducing lilies: in the garden

In this skilfully assembled midsummer medley, pink outward-facing lilies form the undoubted centrepiece without detracting from the appeal of their flowering companions – the deep magenta-coloured *Geranium* 'Ann Folkard' and purple-blue annual *Cerinthe major*.

either sitting on the ground or sunk in it. With gardens generally getting smaller, portable pots of lilies are a godsend, being easy to grow and so effective.

Lilies are one of the most glamorous 'stars' of our beds and borders, viewed as we move around the garden or seen from the house, and a group of lilies brings the garden to life. While there may be places in the garden where bulbs of new cultivars can be tried out and assessed, they may not be expected to play a major part in the overall garden design. But in the garden proper we can plan with some forethought and here boldness can often be our watchword. Lilies are no shrinking violets – even a very few bulbs will make a major impact on the garden scene. Soil, light and shelter will all influence the end result in the first season and this can extend into the displays of future years. It is one of the pleasing features of horticulture that there are no absolutes of design or technique. However, a few suggestions may save us from some pitfalls and our plant celebrities will definitely benefit from careful handling.

There is certainly no harm in planting single bulbs of cultivars and they can be exciting growing among other plants. But we are likely to derive greater benefit from a few bold plantings than from the scattered contribution of singletons. This does not mean that we need deprive ourselves of a wide selection of lilies, because by choosing cultivars that bloom at different periods we can afford relatively close plantings without conflicts of colour or habit that are likely to irritate us.

We encounter a mathematical enigma here. If we plant a group of three lilies, few would doubt that the resulting effect is far more than three times that of the singleton. A group of five or more will be even more beguiling. By the same token, the planting of mixed cultivars is likely to be less successful than separate groups of different kinds. Each cultivar has its own character, height and flowering period; plants from mixed bags of bulbs could well be of varying heights and flowering periods, reducing the overall effect.

stars of the border

There are types of lily for all situations, the colours and forms are various and most are inexpensive plants. While some writers may be dogmatic about colour planning in the garden, such exposition is often of limited value since some people simply enjoy certain colours more than others. In general, yellows, oranges and reds tend to be rather more extrovert in the garden than whites, creams and pinks. Nature seems to ensure that most colours can live together and there are certain combinations that seem complementary. For example, the vibrant maroons, purples and magentas of geranium species can highlight neighbouring lilies that are white, cream or yellow. And the drama of orange and red lilies will be even further highlighted by the soft greens of ferns, grasses and other plants. But to start listing lily cultivars and other flowering plants as boon companions is a little like backing horses – luck enters into the equation. The same cultivar may bloom at a slightly different time each year and miss its planned cue.

A SUCCESSION OF BLOOM

Some thought towards providing a succession of lily blooms, on the other hand, really does pay dividends. There are early-flowering species and some Asiatic cultivars that bloom at the end of spring. Others, especially the Asiatics, will be handed the baton to see summer well into its reign. Then the Trumpets begin their fanfare towards midsummer, before most of the Orientals in the open garden amaze us with their flowers. Later-flowering Orientals then take us into autumn.

Bulbs raised in pots can bring earlier flowers with some manipulation of their environments and, with a little more care, the performance of others can be retarded. Delaying bloom is certainly trickier than forcing bulbs into earlier flower. As a rule of thumb, one can assume that potted bulbs will come

Orange Asiatic lilies (above) join the extrovert, hot-coloured display of dahlias and chrysanthemums, offset by the sword-like foliage of irises and crocosmias.

There is a large number of golden Asiatics (opposite) that grow very easily and are good mixers, their yellow colour echoed here by tall foxtail lilies (*Eremurus*).

into bloom 100 days, or approximately 14 weeks, after planting. This applies to culture in a protected, frost-free environment but without undue heat. To delay flowering, the most practical method is simply to plant later. Bulbs can be kept in limbo by being stored in cool conditions such as the domestic refrigerator – but not in a deep-freeze compartment. Ensure that the stored bulbs are free of disease, plump and a reasonable size before placing them in store. Avoid bulbs showing any signs of growth, such as shoots emerging from the bulb. It would be wise to dip them in systemic fungicide prior to storing and allow them to become more or less dry before their 'hibernation'. With an occasional check, it should be possible to keep the bulbs in store for several weeks or even months before planting.

Without any manipulation, in the garden the earliest lilies into bloom will include *L. pyrenaicum* and *L. bulbiferum*, followed by such cultivars as 'Red Carpet', 'Fire King' and 'Harmony'. Many Asiatics will quickly follow and then Trumpets such as *L. regale*, Golden Splendor Group and Pink Perfection Group start a prolonged display. Few gardens with any pretensions to an interest in lilies will be without the highly scented *L. regale*, perhaps the favourite of the species with gardeners in temperate regions. Asiatics overlap the flowering period of the Trumpets, and some of the standard kinds will be augmented by more unusual ones, such as the semi-double 'Fata Morgana' which can be in bloom for a prolonged period. Later Asiatics will include 'Grand Cru' and one of the latest-flowering of all, Yellow Blaze Group. The Orientals cover a long period with some, like 'Mona Lisa', opening relatively early, while those closer to *L. speciosum* are likely to bloom later, 'Journey's End' being one.

SOILS AND SITES

Soils are important. The most important feature of lily-friendly soils is drainage, or more specifically a soil structure that is open with plenty of air in it and thus well drained. Most lily types revel in soil rich in humus; leaf-mould and well-made composts are much appreciated, though unrotted farmyard manure will not be welcome. Humus-rich conditions are likely to result in soils that are either neutral

or slightly acid, which is exactly what the majority of lilies like. Most Asiatics and Trumpets are tolerant of some lime, especially if there is humus in the soil. The one group that finds lime impossible is the Orientals, the progeny of lime-hating *L. speciosum* and *L. auratum*, and to them lime is fatal. The Japanese *L. speciosum* can be lovely in neutral soils or ones on the acid side of the pH spectrum but impossible where there is free lime. Preparing soil for lilies is usually a matter of thorough digging and incorporating generous quantities of well-rotted organic matter. Do not be deterred if growing lilies on heavy clays or other soils that might seem unpromising (for more information on soils, see pages 130–2).

In borders it is usual to plant taller lilies towards the back of a border, or in the middle of island beds, with the dwarfer kinds placed nearer the front. This is not an absolute rule and there may be sites where you want to have an impressive stand of *L. regale* or another of the Trumpets much closer to the front, to emphasize their size and provide a formidable punctuation point.

While it is now more usual to deploy lilies in an integrated garden scheme, in the past some fanciers provided their bulbs with a special lily bed. This is still done by some growers. It has the advantage of allowing you to organize the site to meet the plants' requirements as exactly as possible. One feature of such beds is that the sides are often built up so that the soil level is higher than the surrounding ground, making the all-important drainage easier to manage. The soil can be enriched with well-rotted compost and grit can be added to make the whole bed an approximation of the mix one might arrange in a pot or other container. It may also be rather easier to monitor the health of plants and deal with diseases and pests in these privileged surroundings.

Examples of Pink Perfection Group (above) are impressive in size, colour and form and create a highly scented display in any garden.

In a romantic association (opposite), the fragrant *L. regale* is seen with herbaceous perennials *Stachys byzantina* and delphiniums.

ASSOCIATION WITH OTHER PLANTS

Lilies are good mixers. They enjoy company. Their gregarious nature is displayed both in the rather theatrical environment of potted plants on the patio and when growing in garden borders or naturalized in wilder areas. This is not to say that they are jungle plants; what they enjoy is to have some shade from other plants around their roots but to have much of their foliage as well as their flowerheads

In the lee of the shrub *Hydrangea arborescens* 'Annabel' scented white *L. regale* open their trumpet blooms alongside the thistle-like *Eryngium giganteum*, feverfew (*Tanacetum parthenium*) and the shapely heads of dying alliums.

rejoicing in the air and sunshine. No snobbery is effected – they will be perfectly happy with annuals such as love-in-a-mist (*Nigella*), cornflower (*Centaurea cyanus*), larkspur (*Consolida ambigua*) or candytuft (*Iberis umbellata*). When bulbs are planted in the autumn or early spring, seed of annuals can be scattered over the site to provide company and extra flowers, and these simple annuals will be happy to act as auxiliaries, the chorus line behind the star. There may be another benefit of this procedure. The bare patch of ground where bulbs have been planted will be given into the caretaking of these annuals, which will remind us that there are bulbs in place and preclude any disastrous incursion into the soil to plant other items.

PERENNIALS

More permanent neighbours could include some of the hardy geranium species and their hybrids. The flower colours are often complementary but the contrasting foliage is as important. In this respect hostas can provide a fine ground cover of differing foliage while they also cast shade around the lilies' toes. Hostas will need to be housed to the side of the bulbs as few plants can grow in direct competition with their extrovert rooting system. Achilleas and some of the tamed thistles, such as the biennial *Eryngium giganteum*, might be useful growing with groups of lilies. If this plant begins to be a little too invasive, the number of seedlings allowed to see a second year can be reduced.

GRASSES AND FERNS

The popularity of grasses remains high. Many of the middle-sized and smaller kinds can form interesting communities with lilies, and they will always be complementary plants, unlikely to clash with the star's performance. Suitable grasses may be large, like the 2.5m (8ft) tall golden oats (*Stipa gigantea*), with its elegant flowering heads of sparkling silvery spikelets. Smaller grasses could include sedges such as *Carex oshimensis* 'Evergold' with its tussocks of yellow-striped arching leaves, the plants being only some 20cm (8in) high. Intemediate in size will be some of the graceful *Miscanthus sinensis* forms, with very slender leaves. The pendulous sedge (*Carex pendula*) can be effective and in bloom at the same time as the lilies, with long flowers hanging like catkins from rod-like angled stems.

Hardy ferns offer another well-tried combination. There are deciduous and evergreen kinds in various sizes and many of these can be grown in open sites –

Brilliant vermilion Asiatics such as 'Gran Paradiso' and its seedling 'Castello' make a striking splash of colour whatever their neighbours.

they are not all shade-lovers. Some forms of the scaly male fern and the male fern (*Dryopteris affinis* and *D. filix-mas*) are very hardy in open sites and make decorative 60cm (2ft) high plants, the 'Grandiceps' series being decorated with tassellated crests. The lady fern (*Athyrium filix-femina*) is as hardy and very graceful; there are a number of smaller forms. Indeed, the number of good ferns is legion.

SHRUBS

Shrubs are natural lily allies. In the wild they are often closely associated, many lilies finding the shrubs a help in terms of support and protection from weather and animal predations. In the garden they are also useful, perhaps giving some frost protection early on and always lending each other distinction. The only possible snag is that some shrubs grow surprisingly fast, quick enough to sometimes smother lilies. But this should not prove too great a problem – threatened bulbs can simply be moved at the end of the growing season.

The root systems of shrubs help to structure the soil and will aid drainage. Soil water will be allowed to drain downwards and the shrubs will be taking up a lot of moisture, helping to even out the moisture content of the soil mass. On the whole this will be helpful to the bulbs, which enjoy a ready supply of water through their growing period but are chary of excesses through the more dormant months of winter.

Rhododendrons and lilies is a well-established partnership, the shrubs enjoying a soil free of lime and this being very acceptable to the bulbs as well. Camellias can join the party. These shrubs will be far enough away not to inconvenience the bulbs' extrovert rooting system and they will have finished their flowering well before the lilies perform. The dark evergreen foliage of both these shrubs adds gravitas to the ensemble. The medium-sized spiraeas, *Brachyglottis* (*Senecio*) and forms of *Viburnum* are other obvious friendly companions. It is difficult to think of any shrubs, both evergreen and deciduous, that do not go well with our lilies.

There are few plants to avoid altogether, but I would certainly be careful in siting daylilies (*Hemerocallis*) too close. The flowers are lily-shaped and often in similar enough colours to cause some slight visual confusion. It is far better to have contrasting floral and foliar effects. Nor would one want fast-encroaching neighbours such as vigorous asters that could overwhelm the more measured growth of the lilies.

'Royal Gold' is a strong-growing, mid-season flowering lily, often called 'the golden regal'. It grows well with other plants and makes a long-lasting clump that blooms freely and floods the garden with perfume.

lilies for pots and containers

We want our lilies to be happy but we also want to have them on view. Pots or other containers, being mobile, allow many lilies to be brought into close proximity to the house or certainly in view from it. As one group of lilies passes out of bloom it can be moved away and replaced by another in bud. Such pots can join other types of container-grown plants to make a pleasing grouping, turning the patio into a fully furnished outdoor room.

Lilies grow easily in containers and are far more drought-resistant than most plants, so they are very amenable. While they may manage very well with little moisture, they do of course need life-giving water. Plant growth will have been massive since the bulbs were first planted and watering the newly emerging shoots was easy, but it becomes progressively more difficult to water as the plants grow. Stems and leaves crowd the pots and the plants are taking up increasing quantities of water at a time of year when warmer weather is hastening transpiration through the leaves. It becomes almost impossible to water from above or to gauge how far the water has penetrated downwards. It is far better to have some means close by to stand the pots in water and allow them to draw up sufficient until the soil is thoroughly saturated.

The versatility of pot plants is emphasized by several benefits. The soil or compost in which bulbs are growing is under the gardener's complete control (see pages 134–7) and containers are mobile, so they can be moved around the garden. The plants will be easy to monitor for general health and specific diseases and pests – slugs are likely to find the pots a complete no-go area. Then, at the end of the growing cycle, bulbs can be turned out, shaken free of soil, inspected, divided and replanted, either again in pots or out in the open – or half and half. Repotted bulbs can be over-wintered easily.

Every year there seems to be a wider variety of lilies especially suited to pot culture. The vast majority of hybrids, even the taller kinds, grow easily in containers and many of the species make excellent container subjects. Those that would serve with distinction could include *L. amabile, L. bulbiferum, L. cernuum, L. longiflorum, L. pumilum* and *L. regale. L. speciosum* and *L. auratum* will benefit from being able to enjoy a lime-free diet. Some species are less ready to grow easily in the confinement of pots, however, and these include some of the rhizomatous North American species and those with rather more staid habits of growth, such as *L. martagon, L. hansonii* and *L. pardalinum.* However, even these can be managed in large containers.

The importance of the lily as a pot plant is clearly reflected in the work of breeders, who since the 1980s have been bringing out new

The repetition of container-grown regal lilies gives the planting a sense of formality, while their scent will enchant those who ascend or descend the steps.

In an informal container grouping, trailing blue lobelia and pelargoniums happily partner *L.* 'Arena' to bring a patio to life.

In an informal container grouping, trailing blue lobelia and pelargoniums happily partner *L.* 'Arena' to bring a patio to life.

cultivars and series that are sturdy dwarfs. The value of dwarf Asiatics and dwarf Orientals as pot or patio plants was instantly recognized and many bulbs now sold to gardeners are these short-stemmed kinds, well-adapted to container culture as well as being useful towards the front of a garden bed. They are usually only 25–50cm (10–20in) high, though they can be shorter. 'Denia' is an early blush-pink lily which reaches only about 20cm (8in). This and the other dwarfs have relatively large flowers, making a colourful contribution but perhaps overall lacking in some of the grace that is the birthright of so many other lilies. The range of colours among dwarf lilies is now extensive; the flowers are often pointed stars, but others are more bowl-shaped. Being low-growing, the selected seedlings tend to be those with upward-facing flowers, with a few having blooms bent slightly sideways.

The Pixie series of Asiatics is well established and recognized as easy, sturdy plants that will never need support and can manage in exposed conditions. They tend to bloom early and will come several weeks earlier still if planted in good time and grown under glass. The colour range covers most lily shades from white and yellow to orange, red and crimson and their heights vary between 30–45cm

(12–18in). There are other dwarf kinds marketed either as a series or as individuals. Short-stemmed Orientals include 'Garden Party', with white flowers with tiny pink dots, each petal having a central golden stripe ending rosy red to emphasize the star form; it stands some 60cm (2ft) tall. Others such as 'Mr Ed', 'Mr Ruud' and 'Mr Sam' are shorter at 30–40cm (12–16in). 'Mona Lisa' grows to some 50cm (20in) and is a favourite with typical Oriental flowers, broad petals edged white but warmly coloured in shades of pink. These all have the added attraction of a pleasing perfume.

It would be wrong to suggest that only the dwarfer types should be used in pots and it will certainly help to ring the changes to have lilies of different habits and postures to bring to the fore. The Trumpets, such as *L. regale*, and the hybrids Pink Perfection Group, African Queen Group and 'Royal Gold' ought to be given their chance on stage. Later, some end-of-season types such as *L. speciosum* and hybrids such as 'Journey's End' will be invaluable at a time when one may be tiring of the traditional summer flowers, which are just beginning to fail and suggest the imminent need to tidy up for the winter season. Take an intoxicating breath of the lilies' perfume and forget about the work to come.

The larger the container the easier it is to grow lilies successfully (see pages 134–5); almost anything that can contain soil will serve, provided we remember the mantra 'lilies like drainage'. Generous containers, such as half-tubs, can be home to such species as *L. regale*, which will delight by sight and perfume for weeks but can also cohabit with other plants that will take on decorative duties before and after the lilies' display. They can proceed to an afterlife in the border, or, if they are looked after, the bulbs can be shaken out before the winter and repotted, perhaps removing smaller offspring to be grown on for a season in a nursery spot.

Having safely planted bulbs in a large container, one is left with what looks like empty compost crying out for plants. We have the choice of adding some other forms of plant life through which the lilies will grow or allowing the pot to be devoted to the culture of lilies alone. Larger pots, tubs or other receptacles may look better with extra plants even if these are of modest demeanour. Trailing lobelia or other small bedding annuals can cover the soil and take away some of the pot's starkness, while providing interest and beauty before and after the drama of the lily flowers. They can also help to shade the soil, cover the bulbs and maintain a more equable temperature. Marguerites, grasses, ivies and all the flowering plants associated with hanging baskets can be called on for this auxiliary service. Scented-leaved pelargoniums' much-divided leaves can be effective in their own right and make a real contrast to the lilies.

Someone new to lilies will almost always try them first in pots, but after flowering the entire potful of lilies may be introduced into the garden border.

The vivid dwarf lily 'Orange Pixie' is grouped with pots of different heights containing foliage plants such as hostas, grasses and lady's mantle (*Alchemilla mollis*).

Lilies predominate in a large container grouping near the house. Prominent among them are the tall, colourful Pink Perfection Group and yellow Golden Splendor Group.

Potted lilies can be extremely useful in the wider garden context, especially when herbaceous plants are past their best. They need not be restricted to the greenhouse, conservatory or patio but can be introduced between shrubs or elsewhere in borders to enliven the scene. The pot can either be placed on the ground or sunk into the soil to look more natural. Oriental poppies, for example, are splendid in bloom but when cut away after flowering may leave a considerable gap – but a pot of lilies will fill the vacuum. They may also add colour to areas that are all foliage until late in the year. Japanese anemones (*Anemone* × *hybrida*) are usually late into flower and you may be able to squeeze a pot of lilies in among them to brighten the picture. This lesson has been learnt in many public gardens. On Monday the garden may appear all right but on Tuesday it is transformed with the excitement of lilies just coming into bloom. They look completely natural and as if they have been developing in their stations since the spring. Much of gardening is about cheating or, rather, stage management and manipulation.

'WAITING ROOMS'

Space in our smaller gardens is always at a premium and we want to make the most of what we have. The patio and areas close to the house are for our own enjoyment, often an important adjunct to the living area of the house, where we can take our ease or enjoy a cup of coffee or a glass of wine. At their peak, our lilies, in brilliant colours and forms, may also intoxicate with perfume. But to have a series of pots to bring into prominent spots through the growing months we need somewhere to keep the developing potfuls waiting in the wings.

Our waiting area need not be elaborate – a square metre or two near the greenhouse may serve, or perhaps just a space behind some shrubs. Sometimes the greenhouse is housed in a site that has a passageway at the blind side and this may well become our plant 'waiting-room'. Most gardens are likely to have one or more small areas away from the main focus of attention where a few containers will not look amiss.

lilies as wild plants

L. martagon grows with grasses in a completely naturalistic setting. It has grown and increased for many decades in this large country garden where it now numbers into many thousands.

A large number of lilies can be planted and more or less be left to manage for themselves for decades. If the right spots are chosen they will be happy to pay the rent of their space with an annual display and will probably increase steadily in numbers. To gain the most appealing effect from naturalized lilies, the closer we can approach an apparent natural appearance the more successful we shall be. The aim is to have them growing as if they had arrived of their own accord and settled in permanently. Using a single cultivar, an initial group of three to perhaps a dozen bulbs can be planted, then, at a distance of a few metres, a smaller group introduced. Rounded or elliptical clusters will look right; lines will not. They can appear to be taking advantage of spaces between shrubs or trees as they might in the wild. Some will grow in unmown grass, perhaps accompanied by other long-lived perennials such as peonies.

Some hybrids, such as those of the Martagons, are fertile and produce plenty of seed which can be collected and sown either in the open or in containers. Small bulbs can be planted out after a couple of seasons, though they may take a few more years to reach full flowering size. The species *L. monadelphum*, *L. martagon* and *L. pyrenaicum* can be successful self-seeders. *L. henryi* and *L. candidum* may set seed but are less likely to do so or to produce natural seedlings in most gardens.

What suits one kind of lily may not be what another wants, so it is worth looking individually at lily species suitable for naturalizing. *L. candidum* needs an airy, sunny spot where the sun can reach the soil and where it will not be overshadowed by its neighbours. It has several unlily-like characteristics: it seems to enjoy warmth around its bulb, it certainly likes very good drainage and is alone in being best planted with the bulbs barely covered with soil. Plant these bulbs when they are available; if there is a choice then the best time will be when the flowering stem is beginning to wither. If you can obtain freshly dug bulbs – perhaps from a friend's garden – these are likely to do much better than those that have been some weeks in a plastic bag in a garden centre. However, these packeted bulbs will settle down in time and if they do not do brilliantly the first season, do not lose heart, as they will probably begin to shine the following year. Once planted, either as a single bulb or as a group of three or more, they will normally behave best if left alone – five or ten years without moving is possible.

While we know that *L. martagon* can flourish in a garden for many years, it may not be the easiest kind to make an immediate effect. Freshly lifted bulbs will root and grow well in a wide variety of soils, including those with some lime. Bulbs that have been stored for a time after lifting may sulk; when planted they can root but may balk at producing a stem above ground. But after a season all is well and they flower and grow normally. Bulbs split steadily rather than dramatically; any brittle scales that break away will soon form small bulbs but these will take several

L. pyrenaicum has a name to indicate its home but it does well in temperate gardens in various parts of the world. There have been several cases where it has jumped the fence and gone wild. It makes long-lived clumps and is completely lime-tolerant.

seasons to reach flowering size. The freely produced seed will germinate easily if sown fresh but seedlings can take five to seven years to reach flowering maturity.

The Martagons will thrive between shrubs, in light grass or in open woodland. At different times I have grown them in stiff clay, in soils with some lime and in sandy areas, all with pleasing results. They do not seem to mind some shade but will not want heavy canopies such as that provided by vigorous conifers. When planted between shrubs it is as well to remember the rapid rate at which some can grow and be territorially greedy. Wherever *L. martagon* flourishes, you can expect the sturdy *L. hansonii* to be at least as happy and long-lived.

L. pardalinum is another long-term tenant, this kind being good between shrubs and in very light woodland as well as in a border. The taller *L. pardalinum* var. *giganteum* can make impressive clumps with stems like a strong bamboo. Other American species may do well in some fortunate gardens. *L. canadense* is a joy when it settles down and feels at home, but this and other species can be choosy.

Several Asian species can be naturalized. *L. davidii* does well between shrubs and in light woodland, as will the tiger lily (*L. lancifolium*). But none can compare with *L. henryi* for determined longevity. I have it growing among viburnums where the lily's leaning stems are supported and here it produces heads of from six to a dozen orange blooms. It is not only tolerant of lime but appears to relish some.

Hybrid lilies that are good for naturalizing are often those close to the species. 'Bright Star' has much of the *L. henryi* mode of growth in bulbs, stems and shiny strong foliage. Its distinct flowers are wide stars, rather than the rolled-up balls of the species, and are white with deep honeyed centres. It was first offered for sale in 1957 and is still going strong. Other first-rate naturalizing plants are the hybrids of *L. pardalinum*, whose rhizomatous bulbs expand to form formidable stands. The colour of these hybrids varies from golds to orange-reds, all with heavy spotting, sometimes heavily freckled. While many bulbs went out under the umbrella name of the Bellingham Group, a few clones were individually named, such as 'Shuksan', a tangerine-gold kind with black spots and the recurved tips of the petals dipped in red paint. The Bullwood Group are British-raised examples of these American species hybrids. 'Cherrywood' is a notable selection, its hanging heads having petals gently curved back but not to the tip-touching extent of the species.

The Martagon hybrids are a range of cultivars and seedlings mainly bred from crossing white and mauve forms of *L. martagon* with the thick-petalled, marmalade-coloured *L. hansonii*. The first to be named was 'Marhan' – a neat combination of the parents' names – first recorded by the famous Dutch firm of Van Tubergen in 1891. A hundred years later, it shows no signs of weakening. The Citronella Group first offered in 1958 is happily still with us. With lots of pendent yellow blooms, the Asiatic species *L. davidii*, *L. amabile* and *L. dauricum* feature in their parentage.

We approach the choosing of lilies with excitement but also with some trepidation. We are spoilt for choice and each season brings many new kinds into the lists so that the range of sizes, colours and habits keeps expanding. The permutations are now endless.

choosing lilies

We will start by looking at the species, which form the more or less unchanging bedrock, though a few of the rarer and trickier ones tend to make only spasmodic appearances in lists of bulbs and seeds. To look at the species first will also give us a benchmark against which to measure the hybrids, since the breeders' work here has given us a deluge of lilies to evaluate.

A few purists may decide to grow only species lilies, the kinds that have evolved through countless ages. Each species is likely to have become a plant of fairly tight specifications adapted to a certain environment, the dictates of the genome meaning that it will operate successfully only within prescribed limits. Some selected species can challenge gardeners but yet may find certain gardens to their liking and romp away. A more probable role is to titillate the desires of the masochists among us. Fortunately the majority of species are amenable to garden culture, though some may require attention to a specific need, such as a soil that is acidic rather than alkaline.

choosing lilies: the species

L. davidii (previous page), drawn rather more finely than the tiger lily, is an Asiatic species that stands some 1–1.2m (3–4ft) tall, the arching stems having a usual complement of a dozen hanging flowers, with raised purple dots.

L. duchartrei (opposite) is a plant with a strong nomadic inclination; its underground stems run about like youngsters in a playground, and along the stems new bulbs are formed. The pointed petals curve back to form turk's caps, all white but usually intricately peppered purple-maroon.

Within a species there can be small but significant variations. You may find clones that fluctuate from the norm, especially in colour, in spotting, in flower form, in habit, in optimum flower numbers and most importantly in garden performance potential. An early instance of this is the selection of clones of *L. candidum* with full, wide-petalled flowers. In the wild the plants are less well endowed, the flowers being smaller, less numerous and noticeably more slender in the petal. Sometimes forms we are familiar with are clones that pass from garden to garden without reaching a commercial outlet; it makes good sense to join lily organizations where this freemasonry operates.

There is a useful clutch of wild lilies that make first-rate garden plants which can be grown without much fuss. Our aim is to mark the most reliable species, suggest others that are worth trying and to mention some others that could be worth the challenge of cultivation. Picking the most reliable, important species is akin to picking the world's all-time best cricket or baseball team: it can be fun but it can also be contentious, with everyone having a slightly different roll call. This is my line-up: *L. bulbiferum, L. candidum, L. monadelphum, L. hansonii, L. martagon, L. henryi, L. lancifolium, L. pardalinum, L. regale* and *L. speciosum*. Of these, the first three are classed as members of the Candidum group, the next two belong to the Martagons, while *L. henryi* and *L. lancifolium* are from the Asian group. This leaves *L. pardalinum* as the sole American member, *L. regale* the standard bearer for the Trumpets and *L. speciosum* the solitary Oriental representative.

CLASSIFICATION

There are 80–100 accredited lily species. Nature does not provide us with labels and a classification, but botanists have suggested relationships between the various species that result in a number of groups, usually seven, which tend to be geographically delineated. Thus we have an Asian group, an American group and an Oriental group. Other groups are defined by their similarity of form, such as the Trumpets, or their relationship to a dominant species, such as the Martagons. We follow Comber's classification of 1949 which has held sway for decades (see Appendix, page 152).

the martagon group

L. martagon is one of the hardiest and most persistent of all the species. The illustration shows clearly the narrow cylindrical inflorescence as well as its typical 'turk's cap' flower form.

L. martagon, L. distichum, L. hansonii, L. medeoloides, L. tsingtauense
Characteristics: germination above-ground delayed, whorled leaves, jointed bulb scales (except *L. hansonii*), heavy seed, smooth petals, erect stems, relatively small flowers and fruit as broad as long

Lilies of this group are found in China and Korea, with *L. martagon* being known in Siberia and all the way down to the Balkans; it also appears in different places across the southern half of Europe with a little less claim to indigenous status. In the wild it is the widest spread of all species. Plants can be found at sea level and at various heights up to 2,000m (7,000ft), and the soils in which it grows cover a wide spectrum from acid to alkaline. Among dedicated gardeners the martagon lily is a favourite. Once it has settled in, it is recognized as one of the most reliable and undemanding of species. There are plenty of gardens with populations of *L. martagon* over 50 years old and several with stands of more than double this age.

In Britain, way off its natural distribution, there are places where the freely produced seed has floated into the wild and colonies have been established. However, in the garden bulbs that have been out of the ground for a while before being planted can sulk, and there may be no growth above ground for a complete year. But all is not lost – the bulb is unlikely to have disappeared. It will be rooting and getting ready to join the party the following year, and thereafter will be just as carefree as any. It makes good sense to try to obtain freshly dug bulbs.

Stems vary in height according to the clone, the age of the bulb, the garden conditions and seasonal factors. Usually one can expect heights of 1–2m (3–6ft), but occasional individuals may outdo this. Most stronger stems will have three whorls of foliage, with 15 or more leaflets to each outward-pointing 'platform'. The number of flowers will vary from a modest half dozen to several times this. Among my own plants are several with over 35 blooms to a stem, and though 25 is a more popular effort, one stem managed to reach 50. These flowers are held by shortish ascending flower stalks so that the overall effect is of a column of bloom rather than a pyramid. The flowers are not huge and are formed of firm petals that curl back on themselves to form rounded hanging lanterns.

Colours vary from a pink-mauve standard to pale pink and very dark maroon. The darkest named form is *L. martagon* var. *cattaniae*, with its colour being made more effective by the unusual lacquered finish – most martagons use matt paint. Albinos are treasured; they shine out and help to highlight the other colour shades. *L. martagon* var. *album* is usually a uniform snowy white but may be decorated with the spotting that is a feature of the coloured forms. Pink spotting is typical of the white *L. martagon* var. *albiflorum*. The protruding anthers and stigmas add grace.

L. martagon var. cattaniae is a dark form characterized by its deep unspotted burgundy colour, usually combined with a lacquered finish, and its hairy buds and stems.

L. martagon var. album is much sought after by gardeners on its own merits and for the contrast that it can create when planted near to *L. martagon*, with one highlighting the other. The white form is just as easy and long-lived as the type. Some are pure white, while others may have some small dark spots.

This species is extraordinarily free with its seed. One can harvest many pods from a stem, each full to bursting point, perhaps with up to 100 viable seeds. Sown fresh in the open or in pots in summer, the seed will germinate freely but this is done surreptitiously underground in the following month, the first true leaves not appearing until into the new year. The plants will then grow steadily rather than dramatically; the bulbs reach flowering size in five or up to seven years.

One can be a little more adventurous in planting *L. martagon* than some others. Most lilies demand full sun and light to do well, but while the Martagons will be happy with this, they will also tolerate a moderate amount of shade, which means that they can be grown effectively between shrubs or in light woodland conditions. Most soils will support them well, but waterlogged ground is unsuitable.

It has been suggested by some botanists that the Martagon group species *L. hansonii* (see next page) is the closest to what is envisaged as the prototype from which the genus *Lilium* evolved, the most primitive features being the whorled foliage, recurved petals, yellow-orange flowers, erect strong stems and bulbs of unjointed scales. In this last it differs from *L. martagon* itself.

OTHER SPECIES IN THIS GROUP ARE DESCRIBED ON PAGE 152.

L. hansonii

L. hansonii is a splendid sturdy plant in typical martagon style, producing upright stems with whorls of leaves and heads of nodding flowers. These are made of recurving petals but not so curled up as its *L. martagon* relative. They are firmly textured and so thick with their orange colouring that it is easy to understand why a likeness to marmalade has been an almost standard metaphor.

Flowers are of a similar size to *L. martagon,* but with the petals being more widespread and the tips pointing upwards they can appear rather larger. The tangerine colour is enlivened by spotting – if it was a child it would be nicknamed 'Freckles'. It stands 1–1.5m (3–5ft) tall and strong stem-rooting may help to engender the formation of bulblets on the underground stem. Once settled, the bulbs will increase steadily. It can be left *in situ* for as long as it is not too crowded by its own numbers or the growth of other plants around. It wants an open site, perhaps between shrubs, in soil that is sufficiently open-structured as to be well-drained; it will tolerate some lime in the soil.

L. tsingtauense

This distinctive lily from Korea and China
is a robust plant growing quickly from
seed and making a reasonably behaved
garden plant. It has typical erect stems
with whorls of foliage, all in traditional
martagon style. However, it is the rebel of
the family as it displays its raucous orange
flowers gazing to the heavens and with
the petals stretching out horizontally, with
perhaps only the tips recurved. Each
stems carries about five blooms. The
majority of my plants have grown to
around 60cm (2ft) tall, with an occasional
one reaching towards 1m (3ft).

the north american group

a. *L. humboldtii, L. columbianum, L. kelloggii, L. washingtonianum, L. rubescens, L. bolanderi*
b. *L. pardalinum, L. nevadense, L. occidentale, L. maritimum, L. parvum, L. parryi,*
L. vollmeri, L. wigginsii
c. *L. superbum, L. carolinianum, L. iridollae, L. michiganense, L. canadense, L. grayi*
d. *L. philadelphicum, L. catesbaei*

**Characterisitics: germination above-ground delayed (except sometimes in
L. philadelphicum, L. parvum, L. parryi, L. humboldtii), whorled leaves, jointed
bulb scales (except section a), heavy seed (except section c), smooth petals,
bulbs more or less rhizomatous and not erect, stems upright**

L. pardalinum, the panther lily, is a
trustworthy garden plant thriving on
neglect and may well be chosen by
most as the easiest of the American
group of species. Characteristics are
whorled foliage, pendent 'turk's cap'
flowers, strong colours, heavy
freckling and rhizomatous bulbs.

Continentally isolated, with species often restricted to particular areas, this is a varied
group of lilies. They are not necessarily easy plants to grow, even in American
gardens, but *L. pardalinum,* known as the leopard or panther lily, is normally reckoned
as the most amenable of the group. It is found in the southern half of Oregon and
hops down through California almost to the Mexican border. This is a very wide
distribution area which, as you may expect, is accompanied by some variation. The
height of plants varies, as does the size of the brilliant hanging flowers – sufficiently
for botanists of the splitting persuasion (who christen relatively unimportant
variations) to give some populations the status of a variety or even a new species.

The standard *L. pardalinum* is a vigorous upright plant with bright green
stems and whorls of foliage. Flowerheads of up to ten hanging buds or opened
blooms are possible in midsummer, each petal being a golden tangerine colour but
with its tip dipped into crimson-vermilion paint. The tangerine is decorated with
bold spots or splashes of deep maroon, this stronger colouring being more
noticeable towards the base. Heads of half a dozen flowers are the norm, but as an
established stand sends up plenty of stems, the total effect is very pleasing. Each
bloom is formed of 9cm (3½in) pointed petals, severely curled back to form
individual arcs, thus emphasizing the protruding anthers and stigma. These anthers
start life as long purple creations but quickly open to become golden with the
revealed pollen. Heights vary from 1m (3ft) to 2m (6ft), with most somewhere
between these limits.

There is no better example of a rhizomatous lily bulb. The thick rootstock is
amply supplied with yellow scales that tend to point out and up; the newer scales of
the growing points start cream. While the plants can be left for several years to get
on with their own affairs, if you want to maximize the potential for increase you
can carefully lift part of the rootstock in late summer and divide off sections with
a strong, sharp knife. Each portion will make an independent plant, provided it has
one of the paler growing points. The injunction to lift 'carefully' is prudent as the
waisted scales are brittle (see page 18) and you can easily find a distressing number

L. superbum can rival *L. pardalinum* in strength and persistence. It is capable of forming considerable groups with many stems and lots of bloom. It is usually several tones paler than the panther lily but it can be a picture of exuberant health, with stems reaching to 2.5m (8ft) in height.

L. pardalinum var. giganteum is the first lily that I got to know and I marvelled at its prodigious vigour, producing plants then much taller than me – some 2m (6ft) or so. It has a parade-ground stance with brilliant uniforms and is able to grow well even in soils that may look unpromising initially.

of loose scales. If this happens, return the scales to the soil as each has the potential to form a new plant, though it may take a few seasons to start flowering. *Lilium pardalinum* var. *giganteum* is either a particularly fine form or an early collected natural hybrid, possibly the result of an alliance with *L. humboldtii*. It is like the type but drawn much more boldly, its stems like bamboo stalks. Slightly larger blooms are possibly even more determinedly pendent and the flower colours of gold and crimson more precisely marked. Dark purple spots are very evident, sometimes ringed with yellow. Plants can grow strongly and soon form excellent stands. They do well in most soils, they do not object to some lime and will manage in light shade.

    L. superbum is a vigorous plant growing in the same manner as *L. canadense* (see page 49) with strongly stoloniferous bulbs supporting erect stems with whorled foliage. When settled and happy, it is not exceptional to have stems 2.7m (9ft) high and plenty of them. Each will carry a quantity of sizeable flowers which differ from its relative in having petals that curl back to make less distinctive ball-like blooms. The colour is usually a pale tangerine but this is variable, some being more yellow and others veering towards red, but there is invariably a generous sprinkling of large maroon dots. If this all sounds rather pedestrian against *L. canadense*, it does have the yeoman virtues of greater reliability and strength.

OTHER SPECIES IN THIS GROUP ARE DESCRIBED ON PAGES 152–3.

L. kelloggii (below)

In stature and form *L. kelloggii* is a half-sized relative of *L. pardalinum*, as if it were seen through the wrong end of a telescope. It usually measures 1–1.2m (3–4ft), though it is capable of reaching twice this. It has the same *L. pardalinum* or *L. martagon* style of growth, this time with ivory buds that open to take on a pinkish-mauve flush that deepens to purple before senescence. This is a good species that can do well in the garden. It also has a scent, something *L. pardalinum* lacks. The illustration is of a seedling of *L. kelloggii* – an alliance with a related species is suspected.

L. canadense (left)

Long known in cultivation – it was listed by Parkinson in 1629 – *L. canadense* is considered a capricious plant. However, when it is doing well most fanciers would pick it as the most pleasing of all American species and perhaps of the genus. It produces a wonderful head of graceful bloom, with each flower hung out like a lantern on a 45-degree angled pedicel; the petals describe a gentle arc that may just reach over the horizontal, a graceful classic pose. The colour varies from gold to deep orange, with occasional red forms. The stoloniferous bulbs can grow strongly and divide steadily; they need a lime-free, deep soil.

L. grayi (above)

This is a dainty and distinct species whose smallish rhizomatous bulbs support relatively strong, erect stems some 1–1.5m (3–5ft) high. The bells are held at a tilt below the horizontal on longish pedicels that are often at a 45-degree angle. The petals form a true bell and then open towards the mouth. All is a rich orange-red, the inside being more golden but well endowed with dark beauty spots. Half a dozen flowers to a stem is a modest score.

the candidum group

L. candidum, L. chalcedonicum, L. pomponium, L. carniolicum, L. pyrenaicum, L. ciliatum, L. monadelphum, L. polyphyllum, L. bulbiferum

Characteristics: germination below-ground (except *L. bulbiferum, L. polyphyllum, L. monadelphum*), delayed (except rarely *L. candidum*), scattered leaves, many entire bulb scales, heavy seed, turk's cap flowers (except *L. candidum, L. bulbiferum*), erect stems, no stem roots or very rare

L. candidum is endemic to the Balkans and the Middle East. Known as the Madonna lily, it has a history of association with human civilization that long precedes the birth of Christ. Utility and beauty are combined in this plant. It was used early on as a fodder plant, the bulbs being edible, but it was also chosen to provide floral décor for funerals and other occasions.

This group is basically European but ventures into the Middle East and Georgia. *L. candidum* stands aloof; *L. monadelphum* is fairly close botanically. On the whole, none of the species in this group provides insuperable difficulties in cultivation.

The Madonna lily heads the team despite its vulnerability to virus. There can be few sights more impressive than a healthy stand of *L. candidum* in full bloom. It will be manufacturing scent and each bell rings out a benison of idealized beauty, an echo of the impression made through the centuries as a revered monastery garden plant, a specimen in the botanic collection or a cottage garden favourite. It still holds some of the aura of the ideal cottage garden flower although it is now much less widely grown. It blooms in early summer with the stronger bulbs capable of having up to 20 flowers on stems up to 1.5m (5ft) high, but it is more usual to have pleasing stems of a dozen flowers hoist up some 1.2m (4ft). The flowers face outwards and are held close to the stem to make the beginning of a column. 'Candidum' means sparkling white and this they certainly are, though there is a touch of gold in the centre and the anthers are a rich yellow.

Almost uniquely in the genus, the bulbs make a rosette of long oval leaves after the flowering stem dies away and this useful ground marker is kept through the winter – an evergreen lily. With the spring the stem shoots up from the centre with alternate or scattered leaves that are relatively broad and kept close to the stem, but getting smaller as they mount the stem. This is a plant to grow in an open, sunny spot. Alone in the genus, it is a lily to plant shallowly, with the noses of the bulbs just under the soil surface. Planting time is a few weeks after blooming, towards the end of summer. It does best in open, well-drained soil that has some lime in it – perhaps a pointer to why it can do well in the kitchen garden. Once planted, it is best left undisturbed until obviously overcrowded, after a few years.

Its susceptibility to virus makes it prudent to grow this lily as far away from other lilies as is possible. The contrast between healthy plants and those debilitated by virus is a salutary lesson. Try to get virus-free stock, which can be raised commercially from the tiny growing centre of the bulb, the meristem; this is grown on, propagated and eventually marketed. Seed may be available but is sometimes only sparsely produced; plants raised from seed will start life free from disease.

L. bulbiferum var. *croceum* is the best-known form of a species named for its habit of forming bulbils in its leaf axils. Unfortunately this form does not follow the type's lead, but even without the bulbils the bulbs are strong and increase easily. It is one of the earlier lilies to bloom and is a trouble-free plant.

Virus may be suspected if the foliage has streaks of paler coloration, often giving a yellowish cast to the whole. Badly infected plants can have distorted foliage and flowers. There is no cure, so all parts of the attacked plants should be destroyed; to leave a diseased one will invite aphids to spread the infection. Other causes of failure could be long periods in waterlogged soils, or bulbs planted much too deeply.

One of the most important species in this group is *L. bulbiferum*, a key plant in the breeding of Asiatic hybrids. This is a European species native to the Pyrenees, through the Alps and somewhat to the north. It is a flamboyant, upward-facing, widespread flower in brilliant orange-red. It is variable in colour but the standard is a bright orange that deepens to red towards the petal tips. Raised spots are painted deep chocolate-maroon, a colour that can appear again towards the flower centres. The usual form found nowadays is *L. bulbiferum* var. *croceum*, similarly spotted but a more or less uniform orange. The wide bells open to become almost flat. This form and the species itself were used to produce the series marketed as *L.* × *hollandicum* (*L. bulbiferum* × *L. maculatum*) as early as 1879. This was the launch-pad for the modern Asiatic hybrids, *L. bulbiferum* being the cuckoo in the nest as the only European species involved in their breeding.

While somewhat in the shade of its descendants, *L. bulbiferum* is a strong garden plant that grows quickly in spring to bloom at the start of summer, making it one of the first to open. It stands 1m (3ft) tall and while normally happy with six or eight flowers, it has been recorded with several times as many. Polished, mid-green leaves are held away from the stem. It seems to do best if dug up at the end of summer, split and replanted in a fresh spot. Below ground the stems will be found to be energetically rooting. The specific name acknowledges the ability of the type to produce bulbils in the leaf axils, although some clones, like *L. bulbiferum* var. *croceum*, lack this characteristic. The nearest hybrid to the species is 'Orange Triumph'.

OTHER SPECIES IN THIS GROUP ARE DESCRIBED ON PAGE 153.

L. pyrenaicum

This is a welcome lily in any collection as it will probably be the first to bloom outside. Its very leafy stems can be topped by nodding buds and flowers as early as late spring. Bulbs are formed of many narrow scales. They can take a little while to settle, but once established they will begin to form clumps that will last for years. The flowers are quite crowded, pendent turk's caps in lime-tinted gold with lots of dark spots. The species has tended to receive a bad press on account of the unpleasant smell of the flowers, but this can usually only be detected by someone determined to get their nose among them. Like most Europeans, it will grow as easily with lime as without.

L. chalcedonicum

A familiar plant in the garden of my childhood, this is now rare in cultivation, possibly due to a predisposition to virus disease. It is a showy kind of lily, growing to 1–1.5m (3–5ft), its stems well clothed with scattered leaves that are relatively broad and held quite close to the stem. Three to a dozen pendent turk's cap flowers make rather close heads, their brilliant vermilion accentuated by a high-gloss finish. The standard form is spotless, but the rather more vigorous *L. chalcedonicum* var. *maculatum* sports a few spots. With *L. candidum*, this is a parent of the accidental hybrid *L.* × *testaceum*.

L. monadelphum

Bulbs of this lily are found growing wild in the Caucasus, often in such large numbers as to turn hillsides yellow. The flowers are nodding, with wide petals that curl back. What is taken as the type is a rather darker shade than the form long cultivated as *L. szovitsianum*, which is a rich primrose with anthers of rusty orange rather than the yellow of the type. The bulbs are large and composed of many narrow scales. They can take a little while really to settle after being planted but, once established, they last for many decades. Stems can be expected to reach 60cm–1.5m (2–5ft), depending on their position, with polished, broad, arching foliage and heads of five or so open bells of recurved, wide petals. There are usually a few tiny chocolate spots. Individual flowers are as large as those of the Madonna lily, so a head makes a fine picture and a group something even more so.

The plants thrive in a wide variety of soils and they are lime tolerant. I have grown them on very heavy clay and in silty soils equally well. They normally give lots of seed and this will germinate well, though the seedlings may take five years or longer to reach flowering size. Grown individually in pots and planted out after two seasons, the waiting period is reduced to the minimum. Bulbs should be left undisturbed in a sunny open spot; if they must be moved, do this in mid- to late summer. *L. kesselringianum* is a slightly anorexic version of this species, paler and with narrower petals.

the oriental group

L. speciosum, L. auratum, L. nobilissimum, L. japonicum, L. rubellum, L. brownii
**Characteristics: germination above-ground delayed (except a form of
L. brownii and rarely *L. speciosum*), scattered leaves with distinct leaf stalk,
entire bulb scales, trumpet flowers (except *L. auratum, L. speciosum*), erect
bulbs, white (except some forms of *L. speciosum*)**

This is a group of Japanese and Far Eastern lilies. They enjoy open acid soils and
can flourish in gardens free from violent fluctuations of temperature and moisture,
but may be shorter-lived than lilies in other groups. They are enticingly beautiful.

L. speciosum is a leading member of this select group, a species that many may
think the choicest of a massively endowed genus. It is one of the latest to bloom,
often opening at summer's end, but the flowers last well, the half dozen or more
on a stem giving a pleasing succession. Each semi-pendant bloom is hung out
on a long pedicel so that there is plenty of air around – a most graceful pose.
Petals are curved back and are marked with a generous number of raised points,
or papillae, often more richly painted than the usual crimson-pink of the major
part. The strength of colouring lessens towards the margins, which can be

L. speciosum from Japan is arguably
the most graceful of a genus full of
grace. It is a paid-up member of the
anti-lime brigade – even a sniff can
kill it. It is this species crossed with
L. auratum that has produced the
enormously varied and opulent
Oriental hybrids.

L. *speciosum* var. *album* is the pristine, snowy-white form of the species. It would be a delight at any time but blooming as it does at the very end of the lily season it is especially welcome.

white. There are many gradations of colour; pure white clones are ethereal, but most have some warm pink colouring and there are others painted a rich crimson. The golden-green nectary grooves are noticeable, while dark pollen makes a decorative feature of the anthers. This is all in a cloud of perfume over the wiry stems and long, stalked, spear-shaped leaves. The foliage is pleasing in itself. This species can be grown successfully outdoors in Britain in gardens unsullied by any lime. There are parts of Australia, New Zealand and America where it romps away – perhaps even more so than in its native Japan! It makes a wonderful plant for containers, with the virtue of coming into bloom after many others are just a memory.

L. speciosum var. *gloriosoides* is obviously close to *L. speciosum* in growth and habit, but it has very distinctive blooms. The wide flowers – four or so to a stem – have wavy-margined petals spreading widely before recurving, and facing outwards rather than being pendent, like *L. speciosum*. The white flowers have conspicuous green nectaries and many crimson spots towards the centre of each petal, while the dark anthers are conspicuously arranged in front of the blooms. This lily has all the modesty of a can-can dancer. Plants stand 60cm–1m (2–3ft) tall and grow as easily as any of the rest of the group in lime-free, open soils.

OTHER SPECIES IN THIS GROUP ARE DESCRIBED ON PAGE 153.

L. auratum

This is the Japanese species that caused a sensation when first shown in London in July 1862. Thereafter millions were collected from their homes on the slopes of extinct volcanoes where they grew in the volcanic ash. Growers tended to force-feed the bulbs, something the plants did not necessarily enjoy. And while the plant may have appeared to flourish, it could be that it was relying more on the extensive stem roots than those of the bulb which, when lifted at the end of the season, may have been a miserable wasted item or have completely rotted away.

Flowers can be 20–25cm (8–10in) across, wide bowls facing outwards. Each white petal can be 15cm (6in) long and is usually marked with a central yellow stripe to justify its common name 'golden ray lily'. Crimson spotting is frequent. In some there is a strong suffusion of crimson in place of much of the golden stripe and the main parts of the petals are blushing pink. The perfume is almost overpowering.

Bulbs need an open, lime-free soil that may have some rotted organic material added. Additional mulches can encourage the stem-rooting. Nowadays the species is less widely grown than the many hybrids originally derived from crossing this with *L. speciosum*; these have taken over all decorative duties and are much easier plants.

L. rubellum

This is another Japanese species, a beauty but tantalizingly awkward in cultivation. In growth it is similar to *L. speciosum* but the flowers are distinct. At their bases they are narrowly trumpet-shaped but at the mouth the petals expand widely. Stems can be 30–75cm (12–30in) tall and carry one to five blooms which are usually a most pleasing uniform rich rose-pink. This colour can vary a little, with some flowers being paler. Bulbs need excellent drainage, especially in the winter, and would seem to do best in a compost rich in leaf-mould.

the asian group

a. *L. duchartrei, L. lankongense, L. papilliferum, L. davidii, L. leichtlinii, L. lancifolium, L. henryi, L. rosthornii*

b. *L. concolor, L. callosum, L. fargesii, L. cernuum, L. pumilum, L. amabile*

c. *L. amoenum, L. exanthum, L. henricii, L. mackliniae, L. nanum, L. paradoxum, L. sempervivoideum, L. sherriffiae, L. soulieli, L. bakerianum, L. wardii, L. taliense, L. nepalense, L. primulinum, L. ochraceum*

Characteristics: germination below-ground immediate (except *L. henryi*), scattered leaves, entire bulb scales, light seed (except *L. henryi, L. amabile*), turk's cap flowers, erect bulbs, white (except *L. henryi* and some of section c), stems more or less stoloniform (except section b), stem-rooting, stigma small

a. petals and nectary papilliferous, nectary with hairs, seed winged

b. few bulb scales, erect stems, 2 stems from single nose bulb, seed wingless

c. smooth petals, hairless nectary, seed winged

L. henryi is one of the most reliable and most persistent of garden lilies; it will perform for decades with little attention. Not only is it lime-tolerant but it would even seem to relish some lime in the soil, a predilection which has helped to produce important lime-tolerant garden hybrids.

The Asian lilies are a diverse group, ranging from tiny plants to giants, and similarly some can be the easiest of garden characters, while others can challenge the skills of the most dedicated growers. During and after the Second World War, many gardens were left untended for several years, during which time shrubs burgeoned, brambles thrived, and Nature was in command. Many places where *L. henryi* had been grown in civilized conditions became hopelessly overgrown – the bulbs may have felt as if they were back in their native Asian homeland. They appeared to have been lost altogether, but when the ground was cleared the bulbs came quickly back into their own and began to produce their familiar arching stems with polished leaves and heads of hanging flowers. It said a lot for the stamina of these plants.

L. henryi is classified with others of the large Asian group, but it is one of the most distinct and gives the impression of being one of the more primitive species. Its bulbs are large, sometimes massive. Strong stems can be 1.2–2.4m (4–8ft) long, well clothed with long, broad, arching leaves in rich green and may be carrying a considerable load of flowers. Wild plants may have to be satisfied with only one to four blooms to a stem, but under cultivation we expect more – six to twelve is ordinary – and stems have been known with over 30. The large flowers tend to look downwards, their petals strongly recurved as they open and mature. They reveal an inner surface much decorated by what looks like a dermatological eruption – large numbers of pimples (papillae), dominating the petals' lower halves.

The flower colour is mid-orange with some darker spots, liable to fade slightly in strong sunlight. The plants do not object to light shading and this helps prevent too dramatic a bleaching. The nectary channels are clearly marked in green down the centre base of each petal, the total resulting in a star motif in the centre of each bloom. Plants come into flower considerably later than the majority of lilies – in late summer, after most of the Asian group but not usually as late as *L. speciosum*.

L. lancifolium **var.** ***flaviflorum*** is the rare yellow form of the tiger lily, long previously known as *L. tigrinum*. This easy lily has a habit of producing lots of bulbils in the leaf axils, an almost excessively generous means of procreation.

This plant is looked to with gratitude by breeders who give thanks for its huge input into the breeding of modern hybrids, first by crossing with the Trumpet *L. sargentiae* to produce the Aurelian hybrids, and then to enter conjugal relations with the Orientals to give us a new race of fantasic flowers that are lime-tolerant – the 'Orienpets'. The species is also little affected by virus – its inherent strength would seem to resist it or at least mask its effects. Fresh stock can be raised from seed.

Hailing from the same habitat as *L. henryi* in central China, *L. rosthornii* is botanically close to this species and may be a form of it. It differs in having longer, narrower leaves, long seedpods and flowers marked by more distinct spots.

Lilies have their fair share of synonyms but on the whole these cause little confusion. With *L. lancifolium*, it seems wise to include its former name, *L. tigrinum*, as this is still widely remembered and echoes its common name, the tiger lily. This is one of the easiest of lilies to grow and may be the one that first makes an impact with children, who can be fascinated by its habit of providing babies up the stem. Each leaf axil can have one or more dark bulbils, so that a single stem may be the progenitor of an army. Left to themselves, some of the bulbils will start to produce roots and small leaves before they naturally fall to the ground. Here the roots pierce the soil and, taking a hold on it, pull the bulb down by contracting concertina-wise. Larger bulbils can result in plants that will flower in a couple of seasons. This useful method of propagation can be inherited by its hybrid offspring.

This robust species has wiry, dark stems and lots of narrow, dark, arching leaves. This extrovert attitude to life can hold a disadvantage. A bulb that is attacked with virus can persist for many years and the symptoms of the attack are not always noticed, the paler stripes of the leaves not being very obvious. All the bulbils picked off such a plant will be infected with the virus and the same virus transmitted to other kinds of lily can affect these much more virulently.

A healthy stand of tiger lilies can be most impressive. The purple-black, rigidly upright stems, 1.5–2m (5–6ft) tall and clothed with the arching foliage, make an ideal background for the many bright orange-red flowers hung out to attract attention. It is possible to have 25–35 flowers on a stem and, as each bloom can be 10cm (4in) across, heavily decorated with dark spots, the total effect is inspiring.

In its native China the bulbs of *L. lancifolium* have long been valued as a food. It spread to Korea and Japan and over time the more robust forms have been selected. This has favoured 'triploid' forms, usually offered for sale to gardeners, which seem to manage in all soils, including those with some lime. Another form, *L. lancifolium* var. *splendens*, is a richer red, slightly larger, its spots painted with a bolder brush. A double form, *L. lancifolium* 'Flore Pleno', loses some of its sexual parts to the formation of extra petals – not an exercise that I find altogether praiseworthy.

OTHER SPECIES IN THIS GROUP ARE DESCRIBED ON PAGES 153–4.

L. mackliniae (below)
An enchanting lily when growing well, it seems to do better in the cooler gardens of Scotland than in the south of England, for example. Usually rather low growing, it can bloom on stems only 15cm (6in) high but when thriving may reach up to 75cm (2ft 6in), with narrow, dark leaves more or less at right angles to the erect stems. Smaller bulbs with dwarf stems may be happy with a single bell, but stronger stems can have six or more. The hanging mauve-pink buds swing up somewhat as the cup-shaped flowers open; petals are concave with only the tips recurving slightly outwards. Colour inside is white or palest blush-pink. Altogether a graceful and engaging character, it is unfortunately prone to the debilitating effects of virus. However, it is not difficult to raise from fresh seed and, where the plant grows at all reasonably, it is always prudent to have back-up stock being raised from seed.

L. leichtlinii (above)
A less ebullient plant than the tiger lily but an engaging one in flower, with bright lemon or golden hanging blooms well decorated with dark spots. This is now thought to be a form of the stronger kind, *L. leichtlinii* var. *maximowiczii*, with a rich red flower, though each retains its official status at present. They are both smaller in flower than the tiger lily, have hairless stems and do not produce stem bulbils. They grow easily from seed.

L. lankongense

This is a delightful species with slender stems reaching up to perhaps 1–1.2m (3–4ft), or even more. Foliage is narrow and plentiful. Flowers are pendent and recurved, somewhat akin to those of *L. duchartrei* (see page 41), but the buds are a pinkish mauve and flowers open to reveal pink petals generously decorated with purple-red spots.

This colouring is variable in intensity but there is always an inclination towards the lilac or mauve range rather than the yellowish pinks. Some dozen or more curled flowers are daintily displayed in well-spaced heads.

In cool, moist soils it can be rather easier to grow than some species, though in my own dry garden, while seed germinates readily, it has not proved very easy to establish, any temporary foothold being soon lost.

L. nepalense

One of the most dramatic species of the genus and now widely available. The bulbs send out stoloniferous stems dedicated to a nomadic life; they may travel far away from mother before breaking into the airspace above. Then they make stems up to about 75cm (2ft 6in) high but usually well within this limit. Quite broad foliage is more or less alternately arranged below the extraordinarily large blooms, usually one or two to a stem. These flowers expand widely from the base – trumpet-bowls coloured a pale lime-cream on the outward-pointing petal tips but very boldly painted over at least two-thirds of the central surfaces in an unparalleled deep purple-maroon that has a slightly lacquered finish. This is perhaps made a little more obvious by gentle longitudinal corrugations.

L. taliense (left)
Rather like a big brother to *L. duchartrei* (see page 41), this has up to a dozen scented, white turk's caps hung from strong stems 1.2–1.8m (4–6ft) high. The white is peppered with little dark purple spots and sometimes the whole is suffused with a smirk of mauve-pink. The plentiful foliage is narrow and scattered. Most, but not all, clones have bulbs with stoloniferous stems but it is not in the same walkabout league as *L. duchartrei*. This species is lime-tolerant. It is rare in cultivation, however.

L. wardii (right)
When growing strongly this can have stems 1.5m (5ft) high carrying 25–35 pink-mauve blooms fashioned in the martagon mode. The nectary is marked in purple. Lesser stems may reach only 1m (3ft) and carry two or three flowers. The plants enjoy humus and with this they can tolerate some lime. Stoloniferous stems engender new bulbs but fresh seed germinates easily and seedlings can grow quickly to flowering size, in two seasons.

the trumpet group

a. *L. sargentiae, L. sulphureum, L. leucanthum, L. regale*
b. *L. longiflorum, L. neilgherrense, L. formosanum, L. philippinense, L. wallichianum*
Characteristics: germination below-ground immediate, scattered leaves with no leaf stalks, entire bulb scales, light seed (except *L. regale, L. longiflorum, L. neilgherrense*), trumpet-shaped flowers, erect bulbs, large stigma, stem roots
a. bulbs dark purple or brown
b. bulbs white, flowers large and narrow

The Trumpet group from China, India and the Pacific islands is formed of some glorious species – everybody's idea of the ideal lily. *L. regale*, the most famous and successful Trumpet species in the garden, is a strong midsummer-flowering plant that does well in most soils and most climates. But some of the later-flowering kinds, while beautiful, often fall prey to virus diseases quite quickly.

L. regale has held its place as one of the most popular of all garden bulbs. It can produce very large heads of flowers that are rich purple-maroon in bud and sparkling white when open, but with rich golden bases. Their size is considerable and the scent powerful. Seed is produced freely and this can be converted into bulbs able to produce a flower in a couple of seasons on a stem less than 60cm (2ft) high. As the bulbs grow larger, the stems carry more flowers, perhaps as many as 20–30 on stems reaching up to 2m (6ft) tall. It does well both in the open ground and in containers – the larger the better. Its energy is apparent in the early start it makes into growth, but this makes it vulnerable to damage from a late frost. Neighbouring plants will afford some protection, shrubs may shelter it from the worst frost and, as a last resort, early growth can be covered with horticultural fleece after a frost warning. Then all should be well.

OTHER SPECIES IN THIS GROUP ARE DESCRIBED ON PAGES 154–5.

L. regale celebrates its hundred years in cultivation. Most will agree that this is the outstanding introduction of the leading plant collector Ernest Wilson, who managed to find and bring into cultivation a fantastic number of fine plants.

L. regale var. album is the pure white form of the species. It lacks the rosy-purple bud colour but is similar in all other respects. Both forms flower in midsummer.

L. longiflorum

The Easter lily is one of the most familiar of all the genus by virtue of its wide use as a cut flower. Though not completely hardy, it can be grown in the open in warmer parts of the world and under glass elsewhere. Greenish-ivory buds open to pure white trumpets, narrow at the base but widely expanded at the mouth. It is heavily textured and highly fragrant. Seed sown in early spring under glass and well grown can result in autumn blooms. Still a leading pot plant, it is now one of the parents of the important LAs, hybrids between this species and Asiatic cultivars.

L. leucanthum var. centifolium

This is the usual representative of the rare species
L. leucanthum, and one which has been extensively used in
breeding. It is a chaste, massive white trumpet, with petals
opening generously at the mouth and throats widely painted
in gold. It can be autumn before the large purple buds open
to reveal pure white trumpets with anthers holding rusty-red
pollen. The stems grow to 1.2–2.1m (4–7ft) high. This lily
tolerates some lime.

We now turn to the hybrids to give some idea of the way modern cultivars have evolved, as well as to highlight some beautiful and reliable kinds. There is a steady turnover of cultivars, especially among the Asiatics, but that should not daunt us. If a particular cultivar falls out of the lists either temporarily or permanently, there will be others of similar or slightly better specifications waiting to be tried. There may in fact be a temptation to choose the newer cultivars. After all, new lilies will have been chosen for propagation and marketing only after careful appraisal of the distinctiveness of their overall appearance and/or performance.

choosing lilies: the hybrids

'Acapulco', one of a legion of Oriental hybrids, is imbued with all the glamour of the East in opulent form, exotic colour and heavenly perfume. A floral fantasy, it is as perfectly groomed as a geisha girl and has long been considered the best of the upright pink Orientals. Here it is shown almost twice its actual size.

Any emphasis on the novelties should not preclude the claims of some of the older kinds. There are many lily hybrids well over 50 years old that can hold their own in the competitive border and yet others reaching towards their centenaries that seem as vigorous as ever and still well worth growing. Trumpet lilies such as the Pink Perfection Group were produced around 1950 and introduced a decade later. Golden Splendor Group was introduced in 1957, while the African Queen Group made its debut the following year. The Bellingham Group, bred from wild American species, pre-dates all these, being first listed in 1933. Of deliberately engendered hybrids, the most venerable is probably the Martagon hybrid 'Marhan', dating from 1891.

There are important points to be made, first about the overall value of hybrids and second about their availability. Almost invariably, the hybrids will be easier plants to grow than the species, since breeders have consistently selected the better performers. The process of cross-breeding the original species quickly ensured that many, if not all, the inhibitions of a particular species were cancelled out by the genetic input of other kinds. The success of the Asiatic hybrids is a classic example (see page 74). Perhaps the most significant of influences traceable to a single species is the blood donated by *L. henryi* when linked to that of the Trumpets and the lime-hating Orientals. The race derived from Orientals crossed with *L. henryi* or one of its hybrids has given us exotics such as 'Black Beauty' and 'Scheherazade', with a tolerance of soil containing lime.

The second point to be made about our hybrids is that all named lilies are going to be good but there is a constant inflow of new lilies that will not be mentioned here. In different parts of the world the selection of available new lilies is likely to vary, though there will be many common to all markets. Where certain kinds are not listed, there will be a range of look-alikes to choose from. The influx of new lilies is particularly fast among the LA hybrids, which have rapidly become an important feature of the cut-flower trade, but the standard Asiatics and the Orientals are similarly active in procreation.

early hybrids: clones and series

'Mrs R. O. Backhouse', from *L. hansonii* × *L. martagon*, was given an Award of Merit in 1921. It is a pale maize-yellow with a hint of pink and just lightly dotted.

NOTE: Where known, the date of introduction and the parentage of a cultivar is given in the caption.

Sometimes wild lilies are visited by insects bearing alien pollen and this may result in hybrid seed. The same thing happens under cultivation and some of these accidental hybrids have played an important role in gardens.

One of the most famous early hybrids was raised at the beginning of the nineteenth century in Holland or Germany. It was named *L.* × *testaceum* by Dr John Lindley when it was illustrated in the Botanical Register of 1842 and its parentage is recorded as *L. chalcedonicum* × *L. candidum*. It has beautiful flowers standing as high as the taller parent, the Madonna lily, and with similar foliage but with hanging flowers of a very pleasing, soft, creamy orange. The blooms are large and wide, though the petal tips recurve, and the bright orange pollen contrasts with the paler flower colour. Bulbs were widely distributed for many decades but many eventually succumbed to virus disease. Once the technology was available, however, fresh clean stock was raised by meristem culture and *L.* × *testaceum* is still a plant well worth growing. There are still only a limited number of *L. candidum* hybrids, of which 'Limerick' is one, a pale creamy flower of pendent pose that opens early and grows with ease. But there are significantly more hybrids arising from *L. martagon*.

In the nineteenth century it was the fashion to give hybrids a botanical, Latinized name like the species, whether it was originally a single clone such as '*testaceum*' or a range of seedlings such as × *hollandicum* or × *dalhansonii*. Nowadays a group of plants of similar origin may be given a non-Latin colloquial name, such as Pink Perfection Group. To distinguish a cultivar from a Group in print, all cultivar names are enclosed in single quotes, for example 'Enchantment'. Most lily cultivars are single clones. Group names, on the other hand, will be unadorned, for example Golden Splendor Group.

martagon hybrids

In 1891 the mating of *L. martagon* var. *album* with *L. hansonii* gave the Dutch firm of Van Tubergen the cultivar 'Marhan', the name being a combination of those of the parents. 'Marhan' is a true cultivar, a single clone that has been vegetatively increased for over a century without losing its vigour. The cross was repeated elsewhere equally successfully. All the hybrids from the mating of these two species are gathered together under the series name *L.* × *dalhansonii*, named around 1890, the original clone being from *L. martagon* var. *dalmaticum* × *L. hansonii*, a chestnut-brown flower with golden spots.

One of the earliest plant-breeding partnerships was that of Mr and Mrs R. O. Backhouse at their home, Sutton Court, in the village of Sutton St Nicholas near Hereford, England. Their garden saw the birth of many fine daffodils as well as lilies. Especially successful were the *L. martagon* × *L. hansonii* alliances, such as 'Mrs R. O. Backhouse'. A similar hybrid, 'Sutton Court', was featured in the *Gardener's Chronicle* in 1925. I saw it growing at Sutton Court, where it was found after decades of neglect when a descendant of the original Backhouse family returned from working as a geneticist in Argentina, where he had raised outstandingly successful strains of wheat. The plants at Sutton Court had been covered with thick tangles of brambles but managed to survive.

Among other martagon hybrids, 'Ellen Willmott' is thought to be a seedling from 'Marhan'; it is somewhat paler. 'Theodore Haber' was bred from the dark *L. martagon* var. *cattaniae* × *L. tsingtauense*. Its rich colouring is enhanced by the high-laquer finish.

'Komet B' is a robust plant with dark stems and neat whorls of foliage topped by good heads of curled pendent blooms in a vibrant deep orange. The pose is orthodox martagon style but the colour would seem to have been inherited from a plant such as *L. tsingtauense*.

hybrids of american species

These are not numerous, which is a pity as they make excellent garden plants for places where they can be left growing for a long time. They are ideal naturalizing subjects, growing well between shrubs, in light woodland conditions and in borders. The Bellingham Group was introduced in the early 1930s, though the first work was done as long ago as 1918 in Los Angeles. The initial hybrids were from the crosses *L. parryi* × *L. ocellatum* and *L. pardalinum* × *L. ocellatum*. Those with *L. pardalinum* blood were the stronger and became dominant. Somewhat later, *L. humboldtii*, *L. bolanderi* and *L. kelloggii* were added to the genetic stew, and the colours ranged from a clear yellow through to bright orange-red, with most well-spotted dark brown. Of the few named clones, one of the best was 'Shuksan' which is still being grown.

Derek Fox in Hockley, Essex, England produced a fine range of hybrids from *L. pardalinum* × a pink 'Henry Bolander' hybrid ('Henry Bolander' was from *L. pardalinum* × *L. bolanderi*). This range was called the Bullwood Group and contained apricot, peach, tangerine and red flowers. They were pendent, with recurved petals generously dotted. A particularly good selection from these was 'Cherrywood' (1964), a tall plant with widely spaced flowers of rich gold and very deep red. The petals sweep outwards and point up but are not reflexed in the exaggerated form of *L. pardalinum*. They look very dainty and pleasing.

'Lake Tahoe' (1977) is dark crimson-pink for more than half of each petal from the tip, but has a white gold-banded centre and a green nectary; there are dark pink-red spots. This is considered by Edward McRae, the breeder, to be clearly the best of the American species hybrids.

'Shuksan' (1933) is a strong plant with flowers mainly a rich gold, boldly spotted, with the tips of the petals touched with crimson; it grows 1.2–1.8m (4–6ft) tall. (*L. humboldtii* × *L. pardalinum*)

'Lake Tahoe' and 'Lake Tulare' were bred from Bullwood seedlings crossed with *L. bolanderi*. Both cultivars stand 1.8–2.4m (6–8ft) tall. 'Lake Tulare' is a widely curved flower with its petals pointed up, in which maroon-pink colouring gives way to white, gold and green. The long pedicels of these pendent flowers ensure that they are well displayed.

popular asiatic hybrids

'Connecticut King' (1967) is a strong plant that for decades was a dominant cultivar in the cut-flower market but also prized in the garden. Strong golden flowers just slightly more strongly coloured towards the centre are combined with healthy shining bright green foliage. ('Connecticut Lass' × 'Keystone')

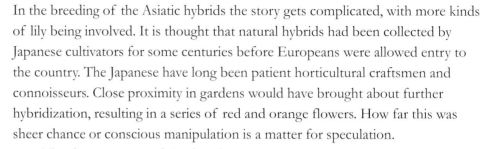

In the breeding of the Asiatic hybrids the story gets complicated, with more kinds of lily being involved. It is thought that natural hybrids had been collected by Japanese cultivators for some centuries before Europeans were allowed entry to the country. The Japanese have long been patient horticultural craftsmen and connoisseurs. Close proximity in gardens would have brought about further hybridization, resulting in a series of red and orange flowers. How far this was sheer chance or conscious manipulation is a matter for speculation.

Thunberg was one of the first foreigners allowed into the closed country of Japan. He managed to get a series of lilies away to Europe where they were known as *L. × thunbergianum* or *L. × elegans*. However, the name *L. × maculatum* was first officially used in 1794 for these short-stemmed and upward-facing plants, originally thought to be the result of *L. dauricum × L. concolor*. The pollen parent is in fact more likely to have been either natural hybrids or the species *L. maculatum*. These plants were crossed with the European species *L. bulbiferum* var. *croceum* to produce an improved series marketed as *L. × hollandicum* from 1879 onwards. (*L. × umbellatum* was a synonym used until only a decade ago.)

Initially the Asiatic hybrids melting pot was derived from species such as *L. lancifolium, L. davidii, L. leitchlinii, L. amabile, L. maculatum, L. dauricum* and *L. bulbiferum*, as well as early hybrid series such as *L. × maculatum, L. × hollandicum* and *L. × umbellatum*. Other species later added to the diversity. *L. concolor* and *L. pumilum* helped to produce a number of smaller-flowered dainty kinds of lily, such as 'Viva'. More important was the harnessing of the potential of *L. cernuum*, the species to which we can give the credit for most of the pink colouring among Asiatic cultivars. While the species itself can be a fleeting one in cultivation, its hybrids are as reliable as any.

'Crovidii' was bred from *L. bulbiferum* var. **cro**ceum × *L. da***vidii** var. *willmottiae* in the 1920s by J. E. H. Stooke in Herefordshire, England, the bold type indicating the derivation of the name. It was an upward-facing orange-red flower. The red, much spotted 'Willcrovidii' was then bred from *L. davidii* var. **willmottiae** × **'Crovidii'** around 1928 and was given an Award of Merit in 1932. These plants are of interest as being involved in the same breeder's 'Fire King', an outward-facing lily that is still to be found in catalogues and remains worth growing.

Working at roughly the same time, Miss Isabella Preston in Ottawa brought out a series of clones in 1929 known as the Stenographer Group, the result of mating *L. davidii* var. *willmottiae*

'Enchantment' (1947) was the trailblazer among modern lilies and after half a century still turns in a dazzling performance. The crowded upward-facing heads of vibrant orange are virtually fluorescent. The success of this lily helped to lay the foundations of the entire cut-flower market.

with seedlings from *L. dauricum*. They ranged from yellow to orange-red and, like 'Fire King', marked an advance on previous hybrids. From the Boyce Thompson Institute in New York came a series bred from *L. lancifolium* (*tigrinum*) × *L.* × *hollandicum* forms. These were given the unmellifluous name Umbtig Group, which had flowers in shades of yellow, orange and red, all spotted purple. The strength of *L. lancifolium* was lent to the hybrids but they did not inherit the pendent pose.

In the same field, Cecil Patterson raised a series of hybrids in the 1930s at the University of Saskatchewan, with a view to rearing very hardy lilies that could cope with the harsh weather of the Canadian prairies. His most successful crosses were between *L. davidii* var. *willmottiae* and *L. cernuum*. One of these seedlings, No. 37.538, although unable to produce seed, did have fertile pollen and was used on several parents. A pale-coloured seedling, *L. davidii* 'Oriel' × 37.538, gave a number of named lilies, including the orange 'Edith Cecilia', and one of the Stenographer Group, 'Grace Marshall' × 37.538, gave 'Lemon Queen'. Both of these lilies were later used by the de Graaff team.

It was Jan de Graaff who gathered together as many hybrids and species as he could at his Oregon Bulb Farms in the 1930s and 1940s. The idea was to use the best forms available and raise large numbers of hybrid seedlings so the outstanding ones could be selected, propagated, named and marketed worldwide. Among the Asiatics, the most successful cross was the combining of the Umbtig Group with the lemon-yellow 'Alice Wilson' clone, selected from the *L.* × *maculatum* kinds and given a First Class Certificate as long ago as 1877. Later on, the 1950s saw the introduction of Jan de Graaff's Mid-Century Group, of which the most successful was the prodigious 'Enchantment'. The scale of the hybridization programme paid handsome dividends – God was again on the side of the big battalions.

'Fire King' is early into bloom, with columns of wide flowers in shining rich orange and stems reaching to 1.2–1.5m (4–5ft). Named in 1933, it is still widely catalogued and grown.

The Mid-Century lilies were crossed with both *L. lancifolium* and *L. amabile* and it was this last mating that provided the bright yellow lilies 'Destiny' and 'Prosperity', which were favourite garden kinds for a long time. *L. amabile* was also crossed with the better Preston clones and these resulted in the selection of a range dubbed the Fiesta Group. Colours ranged from deep cherry-reds to pale yellows, with many pastel shades. They had strong wiry stems capable of carrying up to 25 flowers in a pendent pose. The Burgundy Group were further 1959 selections from the Fiesta Group, with very rich wine- or cherry-red, hanging flowers of thick texture and with recurving petals. However, the outstanding selections have proved to be the golden-lemon Citronella Group from 1958, which are still marketed and highly valued as garden lilies.

The Citronella plants have hanging flowers, usually of rich gold with a dash of lemon enlivened by a sprinkling of small black dots. Those with somewhat smaller flowers usually have much-reflexed petals in the martagon style but larger; it is not unusual to have 30 or more flowers on a good stem. Clones with larger flowers will have fewer blooms but are equally effective, and usually their petals are not quite so tightly curled back. Height varies as well, ranging from 1.2m (4ft) to 1.8m (6ft).

The cultivars 'Edith Cecilia' and 'Lemon Queen' were crossed by the de Graaff team with many of the Mid-Century Group, such as yellow 'Destiny', tangerine 'Harmony' and maroon 'Cinnabar'. The next generation from the resulting seedlings gave the first upright pink and pastel Asiatics. It was the cross 'Edith Cecilia' × 'Lemon Queen' that was one of the most exciting of all, since it produced a cornucopia of wonderful seedlings in all sorts of colours, especially many shades of yellow, orange, red, pink and pastels down to pure white, as well as bicolours. When these were intercrossed, the results were equally successful. The two generations were collectively known as the Harlequin Group (1950). Some outward-facing and pendent clones were named, including the pollenless, pink 'Corsage', dusky-pink 'Discovery' and pure white 'Buccaneer'.

While yellow lilies such as 'Destiny' and 'Prosperity' had dark spots, the breeders Stone and Payne, working in America, set out to breed spotless yellows and managed it with a series having the common house name of Connecticut. Much of the breeding blood came from the yellow *L. lancifolium* var. *flaviflorum*, but other important parents included the unspotted 'Gold Urn' from the *L.* × *maculatum* selection 'Helen Carroll', and the Stenographer Group clone 'Grace Marshall'. The Dutch selection from *L.* × *hollandicum* called 'Waarner's Spotless' was also involved.

the north hybrids

The hybrids bred by Dr Chris North, working in Scotland in the 1960s and 1970s, are fine garden plants, inheriting the graceful pendent pose of L. lankongense *to make them particularly telling. They grow well in the garden and a stem or two cut and brought inside can make a charming picture, but their pose precludes them from being commercial cut flowers. They range in colour from pale creamy pastel shades to blush-pinks, dark pinks, oranges and reds, all with generous dotting. They increase well, especially in soil that is rich in humus.*

'Eileen North' 1985 (right)
This is one of Dr North's hybrids using *L. lankongense* and employing embryo culture to manage germination of the seed. These hybrids are all lovely garden plants characterized by wiry stems, narrow leaves and well-spaced flowerheads of determinedly pendent blooms. Many, like 'Eileen North', are attractively speckled and of engaging pastel shades. This grows to 1–1.2m (3–4ft) tall. (*L. lankongense* × 'Edith King' × ('Cardinal' × (*L. lancifolium* var. *flaviflorum* × 'Enchantment'))

'Ariadne' 1976 (left)
Dr North's 'Ariadne' get its pink colouring from *L. lankongense*, in this case mated with the orange-red 'Maxwill', bred from *L. leichtlinii* var. *maximowiczii* x *L. davidii* var. *willmottiae*. The nodding recurved flowers are rosy pink with spots. Stems can reach up to 2m (6ft) and have many blooms.

tiger lilies

The compilers of catalogues are keen to help customers select cultivars and to this end will sometimes categorize groups. A popular ploy is to gather together those kinds showing a distinct affinity to the tiger lily (L. lancifolium) and market them separately as 'tiger lilies'. This marketing device is not without merit as many do have the pendent habit, spotted flowers and narrow foliage of the species, and most have well-recurved petals. 'Yellow Tiger', for example, has well-spaced, semi-pendent blooms of bright lemon-gold, much freckled, the stems reaching rather higher than the two illustrated, at around 80cm (32in). The Twinkle Group tend to have larger flowers that face outwards or downwards. 'Yellow Twinkle' is rather like a large Citronella Group selection.

'Pink Panther' (left)
This lily has somewhat crowded pyramidal heads with flowers tending to face outwards but still a little downward-tilted. The colour is a blend of buff and dusky pink, being in parts lightly overlaid with a suggestion of tangerine, the whole considerably spotted. The height is around 60–75cm (24–30in).

'White Tiger' 1970 (right)
One of the most pleasing tiger lilies, with neatly spaced heads of pendent or semi-pendent flowers in ivory-white, with perhaps a suggestion of green towards their centres. The well-spaced dark maroon dots add considerably to the attractiveness of the whole. It grows to 1m (3ft).

'Brushstroke'

A strong lily with widespread, lightly recurving pointed flowers of white or cream dramatically painted with maroon marks. It looks as if someone has dipped a brush into a pot of dark maroon pigment and painted lines from the centre a third of the way up each petal, with accompanying dots to the sides. Capable of producing stems 1.2–1.5m (4–5ft) tall, carrying many wide-open flowers, it can look most arresting. The heads take on a more ivory or cream shade as they mature.

brushmark lilies

Breeding flowers is always full of surprises, both good and bad, and you never know exactly what is going to appear in the next batch of seedlings to bloom. The discovery of the brushmark lilies is an example of the unlikely happening. At Oregon Bulb Farms, a good form of L. leichtlinii *var.* maximowiczii *'Unicolor' was crossed both ways with a Golden Chalice Group clone, 'Golden Wonder', both parents being unspotted flowers. The seedlings were a look-alike batch of orange, outward-facing flowers with spots. These were then interbred to give another generation. The resulting plants were varied, orange and golden flowers with various poses and differing spotting arrangements, but a single plant had upright flowers of soft tangerine with bold blotches of deep maroon-red on each of the petals, something that had never appeared before.*

Pollen of this individual was posted onto 'Connecticut King', with its rich golden centres. About half the resulting seedlings had the 'brushmarks', some red and others the much darker maroon shades. Selections made and planted out did not show the brushmarks nearly as clearly the next season but they were interbred and the characteristic became stable. Pollen from the best was used on a variety of kinds, including the white 'Sterling Star' (see page 94). The resulting 'brushmark' Asiatics, which look as if they have been overpainted, are quite splendidly classy and confound the traditional, conservative thinking that suggests that one does not 'gild the lily'.

'Red Artiste' 1998
A bright starry flower of brilliant deep orange-red whose narrow petals are rather more orange in the centre, where the plum-coloured brushmarks are drawn like feathers. This is a sister seedling of 'Cathedral Windows'. Height 1–1.5m (3–5ft).

'Flirt'

An engaging lily which certainly catches the eye, with its cool looks cosmetically enhanced by beauty spots and dark flashes – as flirtatious, in effect, as the most dangerously applied mascara. 'Flirt' is a sturdy plant that increases readily and blooms from even a small bulb, opening rather later than many Asiatics. The stems reach about 45cm (18in) high.

dwarf asiatics
Some of the Mid-Century Group were not particularly tall. 'Harmony', with upward-facing, wide-petalled flowers of soft tangerine, would often be content with stems 40–50cm (16–20in) tall. These were not true dwarfs. By the 1980s a series of dwarfs appeared whose value as pot or patio plants was instantly recognized. They are upward-facing kinds only 25–50cm (10–20in) high. They can even be shorter – 'Denia', for example, is an early blush-pink lily that reaches only about 20cm (8in), though it has relatively large flowers.

One of the most useful ranges of dwarfs is the Pixie series. These owe much to the influence of 'Red Carpet', a sturdy, upward-facing lily about 30–40cm (12–16in) tall, first catalogued in 1974. One particular cross of the first generation seedlings gave a large number of excellent dwarfs that established the Pixies in their strong market position. They are named by colour.

'Peach Pixie' 1986
All the pixies are engaging dwarf plants, coming into floral splendour early in the year. 'Peach Pixie' is no exception; it is a somewhat more subtle colour than some, but just as extrovert in demeanour.
(Pastel Group × ('Connecticut Lemonglow' × 'Red Carpet'))

'Golden Joy' (right)
This is a cheerful lily standing about 40cm (16in), with glowing large flowers of widely overlapping petals all in rich golden tones. This is one of the more impressive of modern introductions, profligate with its gold and a readily increasing bulb.

'Orange Pixie' 1980 (left)
The first Pixie to be introduced and still one of the best. This is a pocket Napoleon – a robust dwarf early engaged in the battle of flowers and the easiest of plants to accommodate in containers or on guard duty at the front of the border. We salute it with its dome of bright blossom. At 25–30cm (10–12in) it is one of the lower Pixies, but few get higher than 45cm (18in). (('Harmony' × 'Sunspot') × 'Charisma')

colour choice among asiatics

Colour is usually the first factor governing our choice. All available colours seem popular but an individual gardener may find certain colours more pleasing or easier to introduce into a garden design.

red/orange

The oranges and reds bring a sense of excitement but may need to be handled with a little care. 'Enchantment' was the trailblazer among modern lilies, with its crowded upward heads of vibrant orange all but fluorescent. Other kinds, such as 'Red Carpet', bloom early and have broader, overlapping petals of uniform deep orange-red, the heads held on sturdy stems. 'Gran Paradiso' stands taller at around 75cm (30in), its flowers richly coloured with pointed petals and some dotting. 'Masa' can be taller still, up to 1.5m (5ft), glowing orange-red and a plant of exceptional vigour capable of producing large numbers of stem bulbils.

'Victory Joy' (above)
There are many richly coloured Asiatics, ranging from red through every subtle variation of orange to gold and yellow. 'Victory Joy' is one of the deeper orange reds. It is a sturdy plant of fairly modest stature at 45–60cm (18–24in), but it is exuberant in bloom, with generous numbers of brilliant, wide flowers staring upwards at us.

'Cawlen' (left)
Here is one of the party-going brilliant bicolours, with outward-facing tangerine and gold flowers; the flower stems anchor the display to the ground but the colours are a vibrant explosive mix more frequently met with at firework displays. This firecracker will light up any border and should be avoided by those of a nervous disposition. It stands 1–1.2m (3–4ft) tall.

'Festival' 1980

This tall, elegant lily stands erect
with almost black stems, strong
dark narrow foliage and well-
spaced flowers. It looks 'en fête',
but this is not a Mardi Gras
extravaganza, all is done in the
best possible taste. The mahogany
flower buds are dark promises and
the opened flowers have true lily
grace of line and form, while
being an appealing mix of warm
pigments, all finished with beauty
spots. The petal tips are dark red,
the middle sections glowing
golden orange but with margins
painted deep red, and the centres
generously spotted dark chestnut.
Standing at least 1m (3ft) high,
'Festival' also has the generosity of
nature to hand out quantities of
dark bulbils in the leaf axils.

oranges

Plain orange flowers are effective. 'Orange Triumph' was introduced in 1939, not an auspicious time in world history, but this vigorous kind is still with us and makes a strong statement in blazing orange early each season. The 'Apeldoorn' clone at present marketed is a rich orange flower and not the one originally registered in 1965. Its uniform glowing tangerine is effective in upright heads of large, wide-petalled flowers. There has been a succession of flowers of bicolour orange and gold colouring, such as 'Jetfire', bred in 1971.

Quite distinct are flowers such as 'Cathedral Windows' and 'Festival' (see page 87), introduced in 1980; 'Cathedral Windows' is also intricately painted. Its pointed petals are coloured rich orange from the tips and for two-thirds of the way down, while the centre of the flower is bright as a firework with each petal having a large flash of gold, which appears to be overlaid by what could be a red feather with even darker lines from the centre. The throat is a rich orange. The painted effect of the centre is similar to the 'brushmark' kinds of lily (page 82).

'Orange Triumph' 1939 (below)

This is a 'golden oldie', or rather an orange one, that still acts with the enthusiasm of a youngster. This cultivar still justifies its place in the most up-to-date collections by virtue of its cheerful, very early blossom. It is often the first of the garden hybrids to bloom without any special encouragement. Its wide, bowl-shaped flowers are the nearest we have among the hybrid brethren to the European species *L. bulbiferum* and its variety *L. bulbiferum* var. *croceum*. The flower form is at odds with modern flowers, with their pointed petals and widely overlapping bases. In 'Orange Triumph' the petals are rounded and the hafts very narrow to allow airspace between the petals and flower centres, an unusual feature. A sturdy plant with shining, broad, neat foliage and plenty of flowers, it stands around 45–60cm (18–24in) high and increases steadily.

(*L. bulbiferum* var. *croceum* × *L.* × *hollandicum*)

'Castello' 1993 (above)

This is a relative newcomer but has made substantial headway in the crowded field of orange lilies. Its breeding helps as it gains some of its abundant energy from its double chromosome count, being a tetraploid. Its generous heads of boldly posed blooms are wide and vividly orange-red. Strong 1–1.2m (3–4ft) stems and clean bright green foliage complete the picture.

('Napoli' × 'Gran Paradiso')

'Jetfire' 1980 (left)

Another gold and orange blend, this lily displays its upward blooms as a wide dome of colour over the shining foliage. Standing around 1m (3ft) tall, it can be planted in the border to lighten the early-summer scene or grown in containers and moved to the patio or wherever its bright colours will be appreciated and help lift the spirits.

(*L.* × *hollandicum* × 'Connecticut King')

'Grand Cru' 1991
This sturdy plant was first registered in 1988. It is a bold, dramatic lily with deep golden bowls heavily, even gaudily, overpainted with mahogany-red in their centres. Its strong colour contrast catches the eye and always causes comment. It grows to 40cm (16in). While it is very popular with many, it is a little too brash to be one of my top favourites. (from two seedlings)

'Tweedledee' 1978
Raised at the Rosewarne experimental horticultural station in Cornwall, when it was breeding daffodils and lilies. It is a selection from the Pisky Group, the orange of this one being overlaid with gold in the centre. The dotting is very much a part of the overall perky character. 'Tweedledee' is a sturdy lily at 40cm (16in) high. (dwarf *L. lancifolium* hybrid × unknown)

yellows

There have been lots of strong yellow cut flowers bred, such as 'Sunray' and the famous 'Connecticut King', which are equally good in the garden, looking healthy with strong stems and shining bright foliage. Many yellow lilies edge towards bicolour status, including 'Luxor' with its darker centres, but others are more dramatically bicoloured. 'Yellow Grace' has more pointed petals and bright yellow flowers with very bold brushmarks so deep maroon as to be almost black, a real eye-catcher. 'Fata Morgana' has proved a popular yellow, perhaps because it is a semi-double kind and a vigorous plant that gives a good account of itself.

'Centro'

A very robust, uniform golden flower gazing upwards and making a bold head above stems well-furnished with quite broad, shining foliage. There are a number of similar cultivars available, some having darker centres, some spotted. Breeders tend to select those seedlings that have broad petals, bold poses and persistent flowers. It grows to around 90cm (3ft) in height.

yellow to cream

The move from yellow to white is marked by some creamy flowers such as the tall 'Roma' and more dwarf 'Medaillon', which is a pale creamy yellow with each petal having a shaded blotch of pale tangerine; it stands about 60cm (2ft) high. 'Doeskin', with semi-pendent flowers, is a peachy cream and champagne blend, with vivid orange anthers. It is a favourite of all those who have tried it.

Yellow Blaze Group 1965 (above) A splendid range of very similar bright yellows that are heavily spotted and have narrow shafted petals so that one can see air through the centres of the flowers, an increasingly rare sartorial point with modern hybrids which have wider and wider petals. All are spectacularly freckled. The flowers open at the end of the Asiatic season. The plants are very vigorous and stand around 1.2–1.5m (4–5ft) high. ('Nutmegger' × *L. wilsonii* var. *flavum*)

'Hannah North' 1985 (right)
One of the many seedlings of the North family, this one displays the characteristic open pendent pose above wiry stems. The pastel shades are a feature of many of these seedlings. Height 90cm (3ft). ((*L. lankongense* × 'Maxwill') × 'Enchantment')

'King Pete' 1977 (left)
This is a regal lily with its autocratic outward gaze, strong stems and opulent golden flowers. These are wide-petalled, pleasingly enriched towards the centre and decorated with a few spots. It grows to 60–75cm (24–30in). Long may it reign, as we are short of these outward-facing kinds. (Panamint Group × 'Connecticut King')

white and cream

The white lilies usually engender a peaceful atmosphere but there are some with more than a little dash of drama, such as 'Brushstroke' (see page 82). 'Bel Air' is a pure white, the centre intricately decorated with many dark purple-mahogany spots. 'Apollo' was a name originally used for a flower akin to L. × testaceum in 1947 but has since been adopted for a pure white upward-looking Asiatic with broad petals and neat heads on sturdy stems. 'Mont Blanc' (1978) came from Yellow Blaze Group crossed by a seedling. It has firm-textured, broad-petalled white flowers with pinkish buds and is very lightly spotted.

'Snow Star' 1985 (above)
One of the best seedlings from 'Sterling Star', this lily is generous with flower and looks good in any garden situation. The flowers are pure white but in some seasons, or in some parts of the world, come with a cream suffusion. It is only lightly dotted and stands at 45cm (18in). ('Sterling Star' × Asiatic seedling)

'Reinesse' 1989
This is a very effective dwarf lily
with good, rich green foliage as a background to
the broad-domed heads of wide, starry white,
upward-looking flowers. It makes a neat, front-
of-the-border plant or an excellent container
one, rarely standing more than 45cm (18in) high.
('Mont Blanc' × un-named seedling)

'Sterling Star' 1973 (left)
This was for decades a leading cut flower,
standing 1–1.2m (3–4ft) high and having
well-spaced pointed stars with very pale
cream shading and dark central dots. It
looks as elegant in the border as it does in
containers. Though it is taller than many
lilies chosen for pot work, it is a mistake not
to use some tall kinds; this wiry-stemmed
cultivar can look very classy.
((‘Lemon Queen’ × ‘Mega’) × ‘Edith Cecilia’
× ‘Croesus’)

pastel colours

Pastel-coloured flowers can be difficult to describe but have a definite appeal. There are a range of colours, forms and characters. 'Peacock Creation' is a prolific one with lots of pale peachy stars that fade a little with age. 'Dreamtime', with outward-facing wide blooms, makes well-spaced pyramids of blossom all in a soft peachy apricot. This form of display is similar to that of 'Doeskin' but here the colour is a buff-champagne enlivened by the brilliant rusty-red anthers. 'Menton' is another outward-facing lily with strong, wide blooms of creamy peach plus a few maroon spots towards their bases.

Tiger Babies Group 1979
The nodding recurved flowers in shades of peach and pink are heavily dotted and make pyramid heads reaching 1–1.5m (3–5ft). This is one example of the Group, which contains similarly coloured seedlings in pastel pinks, all enlivened by much spotting. They are fast-increasing bulbs whose pendent or semi-pendent pose adds to their charm. There is a light perfume, uncommon among Asiatics.
('Pink Tiger' x various Asiatics. 'Pink Tiger' was bred from a *L. lancifolium* hybrid x 'Discovery')

'Eros' 1976
While many Asiatics are of complicated breeding and several generations away from the species with their clearly defined characters, there are some, such as 'Eros', that retain much of the species' individualistic character. This is a wiry-stemmed, free-flowering lily with airy heads of graceful pendent blooms.
((*L. lankongense* × *L. davidii*) × hybrid with blood from 'Redbird', Citronella Group, 'Destiny' and *L. lancifolium* var. *flaviflorum*)

'Corrida' 1998
The blended shades of primrose and pink make this an attractive flower. I find it more pleasing than many flowers with these combined colours, but it needs to be given a good diet, perhaps with an extra dash of potash to strengthen the stems, which can be a trifle lax. It grows to 75cm (30in) in height.
(from two seedlings)

'Silly Girl' 1985
A popular, cunningly named bicolour
in deep pink and pale yellow, it has
an engaging freckled character when
newly opened with its colours vividly
fresh, but is also attractive when a
little faded with age. It has dark buds
and stems and neat foliage. It grows
to 75cm (30in) tall.
(upward-facing purple Asiatic
seedling × 'Prince Charming')

pinks

The introduction of L. cernuum *into breeding
brought a fresh colour, pink, to the range of lilies.
'Rosita', introduced in 1979, is a good pink lily
with dark spots, bred from an Asiatic hybrid
crossed with this species. 'Vogue' and 'Vivaldi'
are similar, but a little more vigorous. Others vary
the pattern by having pink combined with white.
'Zephyr', introduced in 1974, was then one of the
richest, purest pinks; it remains a fine kind with
pointed petals, as richly coloured as many of the
Orientals. It is sprinkled with a modest number of
small dark spots towards the flower centres.*

*Now there is a whole range of pinks. Some,
like 'Chianti', are a uniform soft baby-pink
without spots, while others, such as 'Pink
Speckles', have an abundance of them in the inner
half of each petal. 'Tinkerbell' and 'Elf' are
L. cernuum *seedlings, the first being taller at
1.2m (4ft) and drawn very much to the
species' specifications, but it is much more
robust than the often fleeting wild plant. The
foliage of both is narrow and plentiful.*

'Sorbet' 1988 (left)
A refreshing perky flower in pink and white pigments, subtly arranged and decorated with dots. In my garden it is grown as a group below a crab apple tree with purpled foliage, making a very pleasing pattern of colours. It is a sturdy plant growing to 60cm (2ft), with bulbs that increase freely. ('Concorde' × rose-pink seedling)

'Lollipop' 1992
A startling confection with wide white flowers, each petal tip being painted a strong pink. The startled flowers gaze upwards, their surprised look perhaps enforced by the blushing pink spreading from the petal tips, the shade an appropriate 'raspberry pink' – the best lollipops are raspberry flavoured. It grows to 60cm (2ft).

the L A revolution

L. longiflorum This is a somewhat tender species that has helped to produce a wide range of completely hardy, very robust LA hybrids when linked with lilies of Asiatic bloodlines.

No, this is not an urban uprising in Los Angeles. LA is the shorthand name for a ground-breaking set of hybrids derived from the mating of the white trumpet Easter lily (*L. longiflorum*, L) with Asiatic hybrids (A). In the normal course of events such a disparate cross would be unlikely to result in offspring, but various ways of overcoming the inhibitions of the parents have been discovered and some of these wiles have enabled breeders to open more than one Pandora's box.

The *L. longiflorum*–Asiatic partnership had great potential. The Asiatics have their own strong suits, of which hardiness and colour range are two. *L. longiflorum* has size and a dynamic growth pattern to contribute. It is one of the fastest-maturing plants from seed to flower and responds readily to glasshouse culture. The partnership proved very effective. Any suspicion of tenderness that might have been inherited from the Easter lily was completely overridden by the Asiatic input. The colour palette of the hybrids ranges from white and cream to deep golds, oranges, reds, pinks and some very dark maroons. So far they have been but lightly spotted. The flower form of most LAs has been a broad-petalled, shallow bowl, the dominant poses upward-facing or with slightly tilted blooms.

Bulb growth, either naturally or from scales, is phenomenally rapid. Among my first batch of LA seedlings was an orange-red, which I subsequently named 'Fiery Fred'. The single bulb bloomed for the first time with one strong flower stem. In the autumn it was lifted and 13 bulbs found, each of which bloomed the following season. The average number of flowers per stem has been 15.

The LAs have taken the cut-flower market by storm and they could easily do the same in our gardens. At present, far more than a thousand stems are sold for every bulb purchased in a garden centre or through a catalogue. But the huge success of the LA mating suggests that there could be other liaisons that will prove as important yet to be tried and these could introduce even more diversity.

LILIUM LONGIFLORUM HYBRIDS

L. longiflorum has in recent years been crossed with similar trumpet species to give a number of 'improved' forms. 'White Elegance', from *L. longiflorum* seedlings, has long trumpets narrowing to a very restricted base, the pure white very lightly overcast with green or pale primrose towards the base. There are now a number of *L. longiflorum* hybrids that are of trumpet form but coloured. 'Casa Rosa' is a midsummer-blooming lily standing 1.2–1.5m (4–5ft) tall, and having a good head of trumpet flowers in a rich pink – similar to some of the Pink Perfection Group. A more recent introduction is 'Elegant Lady', which has typical Easter-lily type flowers but with the centres flushed a pleasing dusky pink with a greenish base. It was bred in Holland. Both these plants have the true *L. longiflorum* character and flower pose.

'Fiery Fred' (2003) is strong and free-flowering and usually carries over a dozen large flowers on stout stems but may have more than 30. It has good foliage and freely increasing bulbs. During midsummer it makes a showy statement in the open garden. In pots it will grow to 1.8m (6ft), some 45cm (18in) higher than in beds outdoors. It opens early, and is in bloom for several weeks.
(*L. longiflorum* × Asiatic seedling)

'Moonshine'
This is a pleasing LA, with smooth, wide, bowl-shaped flowers of cream that fades to white after a few days. It is sturdy, tidy and with good shining foliage, reaching 90cm (3ft) in height.
(*L. longiflorum* × Asiatic seedling)

'Amber Light' 2003
One of the best LAs of this salmon-tangerine colouring with wide-petalled, large flowers that open relatively early. The darker tones of the centre lend emphasis to the overall colour and make it glow. Very sturdy stems, usually reaching about 90cm (3ft).
(*L. longiflorum* × Asiatic seedling)

'Rose Madder' 2003

The name describes the rich colour of this strong-growing cultivar, which flowers earlier than many LAs. It is not tall, growing to around 75–90cm (30–36in), but increases well.

(*L. longiflorum* × Asiatic seedling)

'Rodeo'

One of the first LAs to come onto the market, 'Rodeo' remains one of the dwarfest – but this lack of stature does not inhibit its floral efforts. Plants are hidden below the crowded heads of blooms, which are rich rose-pink with just a hint of lavender and with small orange freckles in the centre. To some these flowers may seem to be elbowing each other for a place in the sun, but the effect of a group towards the front of the border is cheering. Height 45–60cm (18–24in).

(*L. longiflorum* × Asiatic seedling)

'Showbiz'

The colour is similar to that of 'Rodeo' but this cultivar tends to open a little later and the plants can grow twice as high, with flowers much more widely spaced. The soft rosy-pink blooms shade down to white centres, each flower being rather more trumpet-shaped than the majority of LAs. Height 90cm–1.2m (3–4ft).

(*L. longiflorum* × Asiatic seedling)

'Royal Parade'

This is one of the considerable series of LAs introduced with the 'Royal' prefix. A robust plant, with strong stems and shining dark foliage, its showy wide flowers are well spaced and form bowls of a glowing, deep rose-madder red that holds well. Height 90cm (3ft).

(*L. longiflorum* × Asiatic seedling)

'Crème de la Crème' 2003
One of my own seedlings and a free-flowering LA with the cream blooms making a wide cover over the plant. The colour sometimes has a hint of buff in youth and with a few dots to relieve any suggestion of pallid lifelessness. This splendid plant grows to 1–1.2m (3–4ft).
(*L. longiflorum* × Asiatic seedling)

'Aerobic'
One of the best of the cool-coloured LAs, this is an ivory shade that fades to near pure white. The shallow bowl form is enhanced by the width of the very smooth petals. This is a good plant, with clean foliage and sturdy stems, flowering in midsummer. Height about 1.35m (4ft 6in).
(*L. longiflorum* × Asiatic seedling)

'Bestseller'
A fast-increasing plant with strong stems
and foliage. The uniform pale salmon
colouring is held until the flowers fail. Not
the most romantic of names – but perhaps
it sounds like poetry to Dutch growers.
It grows 1–1.1m (3ft–3ft 6in).
(*L. longiflorum* × Asiatic seedling)

trumpet hybrids

Olympic Group (1946) is a range of Trumpet hybrids that embraced many colours when first introduced – whites, creams, yellows and pinks. As the years passed, the whites continued to be marketed as Olympics, while the other colours were segregated or surpassed by individual colour strains. Height 1–1.8m (3–6ft). (bred from *L. sargentiae, L. leucanthum* var. *centifolium, L. brownii* and *L. sulphureum*)

For many the Trumpets are the quintessential lilies: they have the form, the stateliness and the perfume. The Trumpet hybrids are certainly an impressive lot. There were a number of valued kinds bred in the first decades of the last century. *L. × sulphurgale* was a range of lilies bred from *L. sulphureum × L. regale*, flowering in 1916 with flowers similar to *L. regale* but opening later. *L. × imperiale* was another early-bred kind, the result of crossing *L. regale* with *L. sargentiae*. The original clone of the cross shown in 1920 was similar to the seed parent but with wider and more recurved petals. A selection from this cross, when repeated by Miss Preston, was called 'George C. Creelman' and for decades it was a valued lily, similar to *L. regale* but with an even darker reverse. Fairly soon siblings and other similar clones were marketed under this name. These hybrids were used with *L. sulphureum* by Dr Palmer in Ontario to raise his Sulphur Group in the late 1940s.

The Jan de Graaff team started their work on Trumpets by raising very large numbers of *L. leucanthum* var. *centifolium* and selecting out the best, trying to improve vigour, reinforce the pyramidal structure of the flower head and select the widest-petalled flowers with the darkest reverses. Having done this, the selected plants were cross-bred with *L. sargentiae, L. sulphureum* and *L. brownii*. From the huge number of seedlings various colour patterns were further selected and interbred. 'Black Dragon' was a strong clone that echoes the qualities of *L. brownii*, large white trumpets but very dark purple brown in bud. Each flower of the first stem of 'Black Dragon' was pollinated with a different Trumpet parent. This

Pink Perfection Group (1950) when first introduced included plants varying from blush-pink to deep shades. It was the darker ones that appealed to gardeners and so nowadays it is almost exclusively the deep-toned clones, sometimes described as 'beetroot' pink, that are propagated and marketed. This remains one of the standard strains offered some 50 years on. They can be very dramatic plants, with heads capable of a couple of dozen massive flowers. Height varies from 1m (3ft) to 2.1m (7ft). (*L. leucanthum × L. sargentiae*)

'Royal Gold' (*L. regale* form, 1955) is usually catalogued as 'the golden *Lilium regale*' and first appeared among stock of *L. regale* in America in the 1940s. Latterly, 'Royal Gold' was dignified with quotation marks, the way a single clone is indicated, but in fact the bulbs now marketed are of two or three look-alike clones. Some are deeper than others with much richer-coloured buds, to my mind the more desirable ones. The real origin of 'Royal Gold' is in some doubt. It is possible that some clones are the result of generations of breeding, originally of plants from interbreeding *L. regale* and *L. sulphureum*. The first hybrids were pale yellow only, but with breeding this was concentrated and the open flowers became deep gold with dark reverses, so the buds were dark. Height 1.2–1.5m (4–5ft).

resulted in a fine range of white lilies which, after selection, was the basis of the Black Magic Group, maintained by the controlled crossing of two distinct clones. This should have been the end of the matter as far as nomenclature was concerned, but some plants were vegetatively reproduced and marketed as 'Black Dragon'.

In a similar manner, one clone was selected from the Olympic Group, which were mixed colours – whites, creams, yellows and pinks – derived from the original mass crossing of Trumpet species. The clone selected, 'Green Dragon', was the best white with a strong chartreuse reverse. If the Olympic Group is found on offer now they are likely to be white Trumpets, with reverses white or lime-green.

One astonishing development in the original Jan de Graaff crossing of Trumpet species was the appearance of flowers with the edges of the petals flushed pink or with pink veining. These were interbred and quite suddenly there appeared wholly pink flowers, some in pale shades but others quite dark. This was especially surprising as there are inherent factors inhibiting the spread of colour through the petals in the species *L. regale*, *L. brownii* and *L. leucanthum*. All the pinks were then intensively interbred, resulting in the introduction of the Pink Perfection Group. These are still some of the most popular garden lilies, nowadays represented by the darker clones. They are strong plants capable of producing large heads of up to 25 flowers on stems that can be 1.8–2.1m (6–7ft) high. In all flowers of this type the depth of colour can depend a little on the season and the situation in which the plants grow. Cool weather and light shade help the fullest colour to develop. All seedlings showing yellow colouring were similarly interbred (see pages 110–111).

the aurelians

Besides the African Queen Group
(1958), an individual clone was
introduced as 'African Queen' and this is
now the lily that is normally marketed.
It is an outstanding, glowing tangerine
flower with the three outer petal reverses
a deep reddish brown, to give dark
mahogany buds, and the three inner
orange petals with a dark brown line
down their backs. Both the clone and
other members of the group are worthy
garden plants. Newly planted bulbs grow
to 1.2m (4ft) but when established may
reach 2m (6ft), carrying 20 or so
large blooms per stem.
(selections from Aurelian hybrids – see
under Golden Splendor Group)

White Henryi (1945) is an old favourite
selected by Leslie Woodruff, a famous lily
grower and breeder, over 50 years ago. It is
a strong plant standing about 1.5m (5ft),
bearing white flowers with rich, generously
painted orange centres, blooming in
midsummer. The wide-open, rather flat
flowers have their petals tips recurving.
(*L. henryi* × *L. leucanthum* var. *centifolium*)

The potential value of *L. henryi* in breeding was recognized many years ago. The
major features of the species that would be useful to incorporate in hybrids make
a formidable list: the obvious strength of the bulbs, its longevity, its complete
indifference to the presence of lime in the soil, strong foliage and good heads of
durable flowers. It may not be the most glamorous of the species, but it has
yeoman virtues and the tangerine colouring is pleasant enough, even if it can fade.
The heavy reflexing of the petals might be thought a trifle overdone and the
pimpled centre something that need not always be greeted with unqualified delight,
even when more correctly addressed as papillae.

The first reported success in using this species crossed with a Trumpet was in
1925, when M. E. Debras in France managed to raise one plant from a cross he
had made unsuccessfully for a number of years, *L. sargentiae* × *L. henryi*. It was
named *L.* × *aurelianense*. By back-crossing to both parents he made a start in
exploiting the genetic potential. (The original plant favoured *L. henryi* in character
but became virused and was destroyed.) In America a similar cross was made,
L. sulphureum × *L. henryi*. The result, dating from the mid 1930s, was 'T. A.
Havemeyer', a tall, strong plant with wide-open, recurving flowers of buff-orange
but with green throats and creamy-yellow petal tips.

The real advance came in 1938 when the de Graaff team grew a thousand
bulbs each of *L. henryi* and *L. leucantheum* var. *centifolium* plus substantial numbers of
L. sulphureum and *L. sargentiae* together with *L.* × *aurelianense* and 'T. A. Havemeyer'.
L. henryi and the hybrids were crossed with the various Trumpet kinds, and the
Trumpets were pollinated from
the best forms of *L. henryi*.
There was a huge harvest of
seed and the resulting seedlings
were sorted into various types,
known as the Aurelians, the
main groups being the Trumpets,
the bowl-shaped kinds and the
star-shaped 'Sunburst' types. We
are still growing plants of these
more than 60 years later.

Of the Trumpet-formed
hybrids, one of the earliest
ranges introduced was the
Golden Clarion Group,
catalogued in 1948. The strain
is still widely grown, normally

producing flowers on stems up to 1.2m (4ft) high. These range from lemon to deep golden, usually with rich chestnut-brown buds, this rich colouring sometimes seeming to permeate the gold. 'Golden Sceptre' is a brilliant rich gold, wide Trumpet with a bronzed reverse and the traditional Trumpet perfume.

A number of the richest-coloured of the Trumpet-shaped seedlings had flowers with a suffusion or veining of orange, the result of the greater concentration of the pigment carotene. The interbreeding of these gave the African Queen Group, a series of strong-growing plants reaching 1.5–2m (5–6ft) and carrying impressive heads of large flowers, dark brown in bud and a glowing apricot-orange when opened.

Golden Splendor Group (1957) is a range of Trumpets with bright golden flowers and buds usually deep maroon but sometimes much less dark. The burgundy stripe on the outside of the petals is more prominent on some than others. They were selections from the Golden Clarion Group. The flower form is a little more open than most Trumpets, a flared form rather than a narrow, chaste shape. Height 75cm–1.2m (30in–4ft). (selections from Golden Clarion Group, which were selections from Aurelian hybrids, bred from *L. aurelianense* × *L. sargentiae* and *L. leucanthum*)

At the other end of the yellow pigment spectrum was a series of cool lime- and green-yellow flowers. These were marketed as the Golden Dawn Group in 1959. A similar, if not identical, group was the Moonlight Group. It was from the first of these that one clone was selected for intensive propagation and became famous as 'Limelight'. Marketed from 1958 onwards, it was a proper trumpet-shaped flower in cool shades of chartreuse and limy lemon, standing 1–1.5m (3–5ft) tall. It is still available.

The Sunburst Aurelians are flat-faced flowers, perhaps with the petal tips recurving. They were first introduced in 1948 and then new stock introduced in 1954. The plants are close to *L. henryi* in habit, but not many forms are available nowadays. 'Bright Star', introduced in 1959, is still to be found, a clone that can grow stems 1–1.5m (3–5ft) tall, but usually sloping like those of the species. The many flowers are milky white with a honey-orange centre and a green nectary star inside.

oriental hybrids

'Star Gazer' is probably the most important and successful cut flower ever, being upward-facing, heavily perfumed and durable. It also makes a brilliant container and open-garden lily in lime-free soils.

The Oriental species comprise *L. speciosum, L. auratum, L. japonicum, L. rubellum* and the Trumpets *L. nobilissimum, L. brownii* and *L. alexandrae.* The large number of Oriental hybrids are almost exclusively the result of the crossing of the first two and the subsequent intercrossing of the hybrids. *L. japonicum* and *L. rubellum* were involved to a much lesser extent. There are now many wonderful Oriental hybrids. Most of those selected for naming are large flowers, most of them beautifully coloured. The colour range is from pure white through every shade of pink to dark crimson-red, often with gold or yellow pigments used towards the centre of the flower or as rays travelling up the middle of the petals. This secondary colouring can be suffused with pink or red but can also be partially merged in or completely independent. All recent yellow cultivars, like 'Golden Star Gazer', 'Conca D'Or' and 'Comoro', have been introduced via the cut-flower market.

The first recorded cross between *L. speciosum* and *L. auratum* was made in 1869 by Francis Parkman of Boston, USA, who flowered a lily called 'Parkmanii'. Flowers were described as crimson with white edges, being 30cm (12in) in diameter. 'Jillian Wallace' was raised by Roy Wallace in Victoria, Australia, in 1938, a deep pink with red spots and a white margin. Jan de Graaff used pollen of this on *L. auratum* 'Crimson Queen' to produce 'Empress of India' (1953), a crimson auratum-type with white edges. The same pollen parent was used on *L. auratum* 'Virginale' to give 'Empress of China' (1954), a large white flower with red spots. 'Empress of Japan' (1953) came from *L.* × *parkmanii* × 'Jillian Wallace', this being shining white with a gold band down the centre of each petal, plus red spots. These clones, now probably extinct, were used extensively in breeding new hybrids.

In the 1960s the de Graaff team introduced a large range of Orientals bred from (*L. speciosum* × *L. auratum*) × *L. auratum*. These were sorted into named groups, Imperial Crimson Group being deep crimson usually with narrow white margins, Imperial Gold Group being white with a yellow stripe down the centre of each petal and much dotted in maroon, and Imperial Silver Group having vivid white flowers usually with a number of tiny red dots. A further Group, Imperial Pink Group, came from a slightly different breeding background (*L. auratum* × *L. speciosum*) × (*L. auratum* × *L. japonicum*), a series of large, rosy-pink flowers. All these Groups have flowers intermediate in size between the species involved. They are substantially larger than *L. speciosum*, with bigger petals, and these are made more of

'Le Rêve' (1951) is one of the best-known and most respected cultivars. By the middle of the 1990s there were 47 hectares (118 acres) of 'Le Rêve' growing in Holland, a testimony to the esteem in which it was held. The rich, smiling pink tones make it a favourite both as a cut flower and a garden plant. It has been successfully used inbreeding, although its own parents are unknown. It grows to 75–90cm (30–36in).

by being spread widely as more or less flat blooms – though the petal tips may recurve a little. The most impressive clones of Imperial Crimson Group can measure 18–20cm (7–8in) across, the generous number of flowers widely spaced and facing outwards on stems 1.2–1.5m (3–5ft) high; they bloom in late summer. Stocks of these Imperials are still available at the time of writing.

The best known of all the flat-faced Orientals is 'Star Gazer', which was first introduced in 1975 of unknown parents. With its upward-facing blooms it has proved the leading cut-flower lily and may be the most successful cut flower of any type ever. It blooms well off very small bulbs and these are produced in huge numbers to give stems with around four or five blooms, but in the garden bulbs can grow larger, with taller stems up to 1.2m (4ft) and carrying more blooms. The deep crimson is edged with white, as if ceremonial clothing edged in ermine. Each bloom has the typical Oriental central nectary star of lime-green. It is a sturdy lily and can make a fine pot plant.

It was a bold move to call another fine lily 'White Star Gazer', as it invites comparison in appearance and performance with its namesake. However, it is deservedly named as it is also upward-facing, has sturdy wiry stems of the same height, good dark foliage and, above all, wide durable flowers in stunning snowy white with dark anthers and green nectary furrows. 'Casa Nova' is a seedling of 'Casa Blanca' (see page 116), with very large wide flowers of terrific substance and making a big feature of the thread-like papillae and green throat. With upward-facing blooms on stems some 1.2–1.5m (4–5ft) tall, it lives its life in a cloud of perfume. Another impressive white Oriental is 'Phoenix', an outward-facingflower with wide petals and a glistening snowy purity.

The Orientals are frightened of lime – sensibly, as it kills them. They are therefore often grown in pots by gardeners who have some lime in their soils and they make quite wonderful container plants. I enjoy the tall kinds in pots, but there are dwarf forms that can be excellent on the patio and these are the easiest of things to grow. I am probably not alone in thinking that maybe some of these could be just a touch incongruous with their large flowers on short stems, but I try to school myself out of this purist attitude of mind. The trio 'Mr Ed', 'Mr Sam' and 'Mr Ruud' are very short, all about 40cm (16in) high. They have been popular pot plants for a decade or two and look like keeping their place. They are outward-facing, each stem holding three or four relatively large blooms. 'Mr Ed' is nearly all pure white but has a series of tiny red dots and rusty anthers to give some contrast. 'Mr Ruud' is similarly broad-petalled and a shallow, wide bowl shape but each petal is boldly painted with a golden ray to look like a miniature *L. auratum*. 'Mr Sam' is a rich crimson-pink that pales to white at the margins. The bulbs increase steadily and bloom early for Orientals, in early to midsummer.

'Pink Ribbons' 1972
A gorgeous package in the traditional Oriental style, this is a galaxy of broad stars in many shades of pink contained in a cloud of warm fragrance. Like all the Orientals, it makes a fabulous container plant but is just as happy in the border where the soil is well-worked and free from lime, and will be a star actor in the showier parts of the garden where a theatrical performance is desired. It could look a little out of place or even surrealistic in the more natural surrounds of a wild garden. Midsummer blooming, it grows to about 75cm (30in) in its first season and probably a little taller the following year. The flowers are 15cm (6in) in diameter.

'Spellbound'

A bewitching new Oriental, 'Spellbound' has a bold upward and outward pose, strong stems and a generous flowering habit, all of which endear it to gardeners, but of course it is the colours that play the major role. The soft graduations of the pinks, the paler golden centre and the sprinkle of dark spots make up a colour design that quietly enchants rather than demands attention. Standing 75–90cm (30–36in) tall, it flowers in midsummer and has the latest in exotic scents.

'Mona Lisa'

A popular Dutch-bred lily growing to about 50cm (20in), with large blooms tilted upwards or outwards to display deep, glowing pink, broad-petalled, shallow, bowl-shaped blooms, the deeper pink of the centre shading to rosy pink and then to white margins.

They are very generously freckled with dark red spots. White margins, greenish throats and perfume finish the whole. This is a regular catalogue listing, grown in large numbers as a pot plant as it is dwarf, sturdy, with wide, clean foliage and easy and free with its large flowers. It tends to bloom earlier than many Orientals.

'Siberia'

This is reckoned by many professional growers to be the best upright white Oriental yet in commerce, though the lower blooms of the large head tend to face outwards. The flowers are vividly white with a green centre and rich rusty anthers. Broad petals have tips somewhat recurved and margins lightly waved. Height to 90cm (3ft).

'Casa Blanca'

A hugely successful introduction of the New Zealand firm Lilies International, which began large-scale breeding in the 1970s, this is an outstanding pure white with massive outward-facing blooms measuring at least 15–20cm (6–8in) across. Carried on good stems 90cm (3ft) high in the garden, if grown under glass it will increase its height. It is later in bloom than some Orientals. The dark anthers and a greenish hint to the throat make the flowers even more telling. Displayed with air around each bloom they look delightful; while officially 'flat-faced', the blooms are really shallow bowls with the petal tips recurved. Their pose makes them more difficult to market as a cut flower in comparison to the upright whites, but it is so impressive that it often remains first choice for special displays.

'Arena'

This lily has dazzling outward-facing flowers with widespread petals of white but with golden centres that reach down to the throat, making it closer to the standard *L. auratum* type than many; the white gives way to crimson-pink towards each petal tip. This richer colouring is also used to fleck the papillae to the side of the golden nectary approaches. Being sturdy and not too tall, this makes an excellent pot plant with its large, wide flowers looking outwards. It is a persistent hardy lily that increases steadily. It grows to around 30in (45cm) high.

'Star Drift'
This is a wide-open flower of rich crimson-pink with darker rays in the petal centres, and with papillae touched with dark red. The margins are clearly defined white areas, giving extra emphasis to the shape of the blooms. The nectary areas form a bright green central star and the pose is upwards and somewhat outwards.

'Colour Parade'
Although apparently an unregistered name, this cultivar has been grown for a considerable time and is still worth having. The richly coloured flowers are well-formed, long-lasting and are pleasingly shaded a deeper colour in the petal centres, fading towards the margins. It grows 75–90cm (30–36in) tall. It is shown here nearly twice its actual size.

the orienpets

The Achilles heel of the Orientals is their fatal reaction to lime. Now we have a new race of hybrids that combine the exotic allure of the Orientals with the strength, garden-worthiness and lime tolerance of *L. henryi* and the Trumpet and Aurelian hybrids. These lilies are known among lily fanciers and in catalogues as 'Orienpets', not the most musical of names but giving some clue as to their origin, the 'pets' being lopped off the word trumpets. The introduction of this foreign blood has produced plants of outstanding garden worth that are strong, reliable and improving year after year. They bloom towards the end of the lily season, are at their best in late summer and can have many large, thick-textured flowers in succession. This breeding phenomenon is one of the biggest advances in the history of lily breeding.

The Orienpets look set to take a leading part in the lily cult, but they are going to do more than this. They will appeal to gardeners with more general interests, as the plants and flowers are very impressive and come into bloom in the second half of summer, when other plants have begun to tire and something fresh and distinctive is especially welcome in the garden.

'Arabesque'
Bred by Peter Schenk in Holland, this is a hugely vigorous plant with massively strong stems 1.2–1.8m (4–6ft) high. It has large, elegant flat flowers of rich crimson-red, though the petal tips are touched with white and recurve. The petals are impressively wide-spread to make the most of their colours. The blooms face outwards in wide heads, a very attractive and effective pose, so that a group of three bulbs can give the impression of far more. The bulbs increase steadily. Height 1–1.2m (3–4ft).
('Tetra Black Beauty' × 'Tetra Journey's End')

'Scheherazade' (left)
Always making a big impression, this
has proved one of the most popular
of the Orienpets with gardeners in
the US and elsewhere. Bred from the
yellow Aurelian 'Thunderbolt' × 'Tetra
Black Beauty', 'Scheherazade' is a
fantastic plant with many pendent
crimson and white flowers, wider than
those of 'Black Beauty' but with tips
recurving. The prominent green
nectary stars are surrounded by the
dominant dark crimson with only
narrow margins and tips of white.
Bulbs of this fantastic Orienpet
should be sold with ladders. The first
year it may be 1–1.8m (3–5ft) tall, but
established plants will be much taller.
We have had stems well over 2.7m (9ft)
high, with 40 or more blooms on each.

'Black Beauty' 1957 (right)
This is an outstanding garden lily,
the first of the lime-tolerant
Orienpets to take its place in
catalogues and in gardens. It has
very recurved, speciosum-type
flowers of dark crimson, a 'black-
red' that is enlivened by very narrow
white margins. The green star centre
is prominent. It stands some
1–1.5m (3–5ft) high with sloping
stems and many semi-pendent
blooms. It is a prodigy of vigour.
As the bulbs establish themselves,
the payload of the stems increases –
50 is fairly normal, 100 is perfectly
possible and 150 is not unknown!
This clone is a sterile one, but a
fertile one giving seed and viable
pollen was artificially produced, a
tetraploid kind marketed as 'Tetra
Black Beauty'. It is similar but of
even firmer texture.
(*L. speciosum* var. *rubrum* × *L. henryi*)

'Silk Road' (left)
Another gutsy Orienpet, this time with trumpet genes showing some influence in the form of the flowers which are flared, deep bowl-trumpets rather than the 'starry' or recurved forms of most others. Perhaps we can also detect trumpet influence in the perfume and in the substantial size of the large, long buds. It is a tall, strong plant that blooms earlier than most of its relatives. The large, heavily perfumed flowers form wide bowls which are a rich crimson-pink, becoming darker towards the centre but white at the margins and tips. These blooms face outwards or tilt slightly downwards. Each season sees an increase in the size of the bulb, the stem and the number of flowers. It grows to 1.2–1.8m (4–6ft) tall.

'Catherine the Great' (right)
This is at present the leading yellow Orienpet. Strong stems up to 1.8m (6ft) tall hold spaced heads of large flowers that face outwards. The trumpet ancestry can be seen in the stems, foliage and large bud forms as well as in the yellow pigments of the flowers. In bud and while opening they could be taken to be trumpets but they open widely to form wide bowls of thick-textured, slightly ruffled petals. The flowers are held more or less horizontally and are quite late into bloom. The colour is normally a cool primrose with darker, more golden tones towards the centre and base of each petal; the margins can look nearly white in some seasons. The cooler the weather, the deeper are the primrose-gold shades.

The dynamic, exotic-looking lily genus is one of the most exciting features of contemporary horticulture. And while exotic things are attractive, they often suggest difficulty. But any such fears about lilies will be banished by this practical, straightforward guide to planting and cultivation.

growing lilies

Lilies are in many ways the ideal gardener's hobby plant, being one that will respond to the restricted care of a busy person but also one that will reward extra study and can offer a series of challenges. The range of interesting propagation methods will delight many gardeners and those growers who venture into breeding their own cultivars are likely to be lost to more staid pursuits.

The hybridization of lilies has successfully overcome any inhibitions that the species might have about taking to cultivation to such a happy extent that lilies have become one of the easiest of garden plants to grow and to propagate. They are certainly the most straightforward and trouble-free bulbs to grow as container plants, being far more amenable than daffodils, tulips, hyacinths and other bulbs. Before planting your lilies, it is as well to understand their life cycle, or how they will behave throughout the year.

growing lilies: planting

Lilies enjoy well-drained and cultivated soils that are neutral or slightly acid. The addition of rotted organic matter will improve soil fertility and help to maintain an open, fibrous mix.

CYCLE OF GROWTH

Bulbs planted in early autumn or early spring get into action quickly, with roots emerging from the basal plate of the bulb and in the spring a stem rising towards the soil surface. In the majority of lilies this stem gives rises to its own system of roots, usually in rings that are pressing outwards even as the stem reaches for the surface. The stem produces its quota of leaves, sometimes a huge number but in some kinds only a sparse scattering. Flowers may number from a singleton to over 150 per stem! After the flowers have faded, seedpods may develop. These will split vertically to allow the flat disc-like seeds to float away from each of the three chambers, each chamber having two piles of seeds. By now the plant has begun to wind down for the winter 'dormant' months, and leaves and stem turn pale brown.

The end of summer will be the time to lift early-flowering lilies if they are due to be split up and given more room. Later-flowering kinds can be lifted some weeks before the onset of winter weather. The idea is to replant immediately in pots or in the open and allow the bulbs to begin to form a new rooting system before the colder, wetter weather. Frosty conditions combined with wet can be particularly bad for lilies in pots where the frost can penetrate not only from the top but also from the sides, so aim to keep the plants on the dry side through the winter.

buying lily bulbs

A selection of lily bulbs may be offered for sale loose in a garden centre. Always pick the plumpest with the minimum of bruising and avoid those with withered scales.

For gardeners the most obvious sources of bulbs are garden centres or mail order catalogues. Garden centres may have a dozen or a couple of dozen lilies, while a good general bulb catalogue may list as may as 50–70 kinds and a lily specialist could produce a catalogue with well over a hundred different cultivars and species. The prices of bulbs vary; a few of the rarer newer types can be very expensive, but generally the lower price per bulb reflects the relative ease with which bulbs can be increased. You can order from bulb traders with considerable confidence, since they need repeat orders to keep their business healthy and will therefore be careful about the bulbs they supply. They should be true to name, healthy and packed carefully to prevent bruising or other damage during transit. Some of these suppliers are listed under Further Information (see page 156).

The selection offered by larger garden centres, although not as wide as that of specialist firms, can still be impressive and customers have the benefit of being able to see the bulbs they are purchasing. The lesser number of kinds offered may mean that only the most reliable garden plants are included. Old favourites are not ignored but, surprisingly, new lilies are often introduced into garden centres before they get into the bulb suppliers' catalogues. Garden centres now also provide a wide choice of potted lilies, usually three to a pot, displayed with green flower buds not far from colouring and thus only a few weeks before flowering. These are usually good value, often costing little more than the price of three individual bulbs. Favourite kinds for this enterprise are the dwarf lilies, including several Asiatic series such as the variously coloured Pixies, reaching heights of 25–38cm (10–15in). Low-growing Orientals such as 'Mona Lisa' are also sold in this way.

CHOOSING BULBS

The best time to plant lilies is in early autumn or early spring (see Planting, page 130) and you can buy your bulbs at these times. If you are ordering by mail order, the earlier the better to avoid the risk of missing kinds that may sell out and to allow the supplier to send your bulbs at an appropriate time. If bulbs are bought or received in the middle of winter, when planting conditions are next to impossible, plant them up in pots and keep these under cool cover until early spring when the whole potful can be planted out.

If buying bulbs at a garden centre, you will be able to choose the ones you feel are the best. Always look for plump, undamaged bulbs; all other things being equal, a good big one beats a good little one. As lily bulbs are without any protective layers they are easily bruised. Bruising can start rotting and any brown rotting around the base is a real danger sign. Blue penicillin mould may appear on slightly damaged tissue, but this need not be too great a cause for concern since the small area affected can be cut away with a sharp knife and the exposed tissue

Packets should give the name of the lily, usually its type (Trumpet, Asiatic or Oriental), its height and basic suggestions about its culture.

dusted or soaked with fungicide before planting. Avoid bulbs with stems growing from them and trying to force their way out of the packet. This does not mean that you should avoid any bulb with the beginning of growth in the nose, as such bulbs will generally grow well if planted immediately.

The usual format is to offer bulbs singly, or in twos or threes, in plastic packets with coloured illustrations. Most good garden centres house packeted bulbs in reasonable conditions and will remove them from sale if they deteriorate. Bulbs that appear flaccid may be restored to better condition if covered for a day or two with moist peat or similar material. However, it is not unusual to find packets that have been hanging around for ages in which the bulbs are completely dehydrated; there will be no resurrecting these – they are as dead as the well-known doornail. Packeted bulbs are likely to be of a reasonable rather than fully mature size. Considerations of packaging, transport, weight and general ease of handling make it nearly prohibitive to use the size of bulbs that you will grow from the ones you buy. But at the end of their first season you should be able to see a most satisfying increase in size.

Other bulbs may be displayed loose, perhaps with some peat around them to minimize bruising and keep them from drying out too much. These loose bulbs are often larger and, if bought fresh, will give excellent results; they should be more prolific of bloom than the smaller packeted bulbs of the same cultivar. There are good reasons for purchasing these bulbs soon after they are put on display. You will be picking out the best bulbs. The juicier they are, the more quickly they will respond by growing strongly. And although some kinds of lily have bulbs that look distinctly different from others, all the Trumpet kinds, for example, look alike. Previous browsers may have returned bulbs to the wrong compartment so that some months later there is a chance of you finding a cuckoo in the nest.

We live in a consumer age of special offers and these appear in the gardening world as elsewhere. Sometimes they are good value, but I would not usually recommend buying the mixed packets of lilies as they are unnamed and will all have different specifications. If you are not worried about knowing the names and think a small gamble worth trying, you could plant out a packetful and then if any particularly take your fancy, those bulbs can be propagated for following seasons.

planting in beds and borders

Bulbs can be planted outside in autumn or spring. In years past the usual advice was to plant early in the autumn to allow the bulbs to get well rooted before winter. This remains a sensible procedure, but the advice dates from a time when bulbs were not readily available in spring and the technology to store bulbs for long periods without any deterioration was unavailable or not exploited. In heavy soils, autumn-planted bulbs may have to deal with wet conditions for some months and such soils may have a population of slugs that could attack the bulbs. If you plant bulbs in autumn, it is wise to do it early to allow the rooting system to be well formed and the soil structure to settle before the winter. The resulting plants can grow taller than spring-planted ones.

Early spring has the advantage of a soil that is beginning to warm up and stimulate the growth of all plants. The lily bulbs are likely to produce roots rapidly and not be long forcing their shoots upwards. A few slug pellets can be laid on the soil or other precautions taken to minimize the likelihood of damage. Once the lilies have broken through the soil, growth becomes increasingly slug-resistant. It may also perhaps be a little easier in spring to see how the lilies could play their part in the overall garden plan.

Planting sites should be well dug, weed-free and, where necessary, have organic matter and grit added. The aim is to provide an open-structured soil rich in humus, after which drainage should be assured. Check the health of your bulbs before proceeding to plant (see page 128).

SITES AND SOILS

As we have seen, lilies will grow in most garden soils without too much trouble. A very chalky soil will preclude some lilies and will require the addition of rotted organic matter to keep even lime-tolerant kinds really happy. Heavy clays are not ideal, as they can compact and leave drainage poor, with little air in the soil. The perfect soil would be a healthy loam slightly on the acid side of neutral, with a good ration of organic materialincorporating a to keep the whole an open, fibrous mix.

Humus is a vital ingredient in a healthy garden soil. It is the complex chemical result of the decomposition of living matter, an organic residue. It helps to provide an open structure and so aids drainage, but it is also water-retentive and helps to keep plants going in times of water shortage. It has an important role in soil fertility. The best source of humus is well-rotted organic matter such as garden compost or rotted horse manure.

Lily bulbs and roots will be happiest in soil that is shaded, with the exception of *L. candidum* which seems to welcome sun on its soil. And while lilies appear to grow best when associated with other plants, they do not like being crowded or too heavily shaded. The maxim is 'toes in the shade, faces in the sun'. The growing

L. speciosum, seen here with deep red dahlias, is one of the last lilies to bloom and brings a freshness to the autumn garden scene.

plants enjoy an airy environment; still, humid conditions can help to foster fungus diseases such as botrytis. On the other hand, no lily is going to be very pleased to find itself living in a wind-tunnel or in any position subject to strong gales.

pH values

The acidity or alkalinity of a soil is measured on a scale of 1 to 14 in which 7 is neutral. Higher numbers point to increasing alkalinity, lower ones to greater acidity. There is a range of simple testing kits that will help you to determine the pH level of your soil and it is worth taking several readings from different areas of the garden, as levels can fluctuate considerably within a relatively short distance. For instance, against an old wall made of old-fashioned mortar there will have been a gradual addition of soluble lime salts from the rain passing over the wall. Readings from 5.5 to 7.5 may be taken as ideal.

Practical good sense should dictate that gardeners grow the plants that suit their soils, but gardeners are as perverse as the rest of humanity and will always want to try acid-loving plants when their soil is alkaline and vice versa. Of course soils can be doctored by the addition of lime to increase alkalinity or chemicals that inhibit the effect of lime to encourage acidity. The addition of humus in the form of well-rotted organic matter will help swing the level to the acid side, but it will take a lot to move the reading a complete point; any lime present will break down the humus. Fortunately, the vast majority of gardens have soils that are neutral or within a short measure of this on either side of the scale and such soils will be fine for most lilies.

Drainage

The most important feature of lily soils is their drainage. The roots of the bulbs love to get delving into an open-structured soil with a lot of air in it. Grit and humus will help to enhance such a structure. There may be areas of the garden that are poorly drained and here it will pay dividends to make drains to take away standing or surplus water. Such drains can be made by half-filling trenches with rubble covered with a semi-impervious layer of material that will prevent it from immediately filling with soil. Turf, tree or shrub 'brushwood' or even newspapers will serve as this layer. The slope away to lower ground or to more important drains need not be dramatic but it needs to be there.

Lilies will enjoy fairly plentiful moisture during their active growing months but through the winter they will be happier to be kept drier. Standing water with long-sodden soil will adversely affect the bulbs, since lilies dislike stagnant conditions and this especially applies in the winter. Rotting can start and fungus diseases be encouraged by continuous wet. You might give some of the more fussy species some protection from excessive winter wet in the form of cloches or sheets of glass over their sites, but this should not be needed by most lilies or in most sites. In nature the bulbs may well be covered by a blanket of snow that keeps them from being too wet for several months. The bulbs will not relish being frozen, but normal cold is clearly not something to which they object.

PLANTING DEPTH AND DISTANCE

The depth at which you plant the bulbs and the distance apart will vary according to the type of lily.

ASIATIC LILIES will be best with at least 10cm (4in) of soil over the top of the bulbs, or planted slightly deeper in very light soil. If you intend to lift the bulbs after a season, you can plant them as close as 15cm (6in) apart, but if they are to be left for two or three years, allow 30cm (12in) for the increasing number of bulbs.

SPECIES LILIES WITH SMALL BULBS, such as *L. concolor* and *L. pumilum*, can be planted less deeply, with 8cm (3in) of soil covering them, and as close as 10–15cm (4–6in).

LILIUM CANDIDUM has quite large, rather loose-scaled bulbs and these are treated differently from all other kinds. Plant the bulbs with their noses close to the soil surface as they may struggle if planted deeply, and 20–25cm (8–10in) apart.

TRUMPET LILIES with large bulbs, such as *L. regale* and hybrids like Pink Perfection Group, need to be planted more deeply, at 15–20cm (6–8in), as do such strong-growing lilies as the Orienpets 'Black Beauty' and the tall 'Scheherazade'. Their large flowering heads mean that they also need plenty of room: 38cm (15in) apart would be a minimum when planting for a stay of two or more years. I usually plant 'Scheherazade' with at least 60cm (24in) between the bulbs, sometimes more.

PLANTING LILY BULBS IN A BORDER

1 Lay the bulbs on well-prepared soil in their rough spacings and make individual holes using a trowel.

2 The hole's depth will depend on the type of bulb (see opposite); most need at least 10cm (4in) of soil over them.

3 Place the bulb in its hole with the roots carefully spread out and cover with soil.

4 Level the soil and label the bulb to indicate its position, then plant others in the group.

THE RHIZOMATOUS BULBS of *L. pardalinum* and its hybrids are best planted 10cm (4in) deep. As these are likely to remain *in situ* for a few seasons, it would be a mistake to plant too closely – consider 30cm (12in) apart a minimum. The behaviour of these bulbs can be unusual: as they grow and spread sideways they appear to travel some distance towards the surface. They must find the depth at which they are happiest but it is best to start freshly introduced bulbs with a 10cm (4in) cover of soil. This keeps them cool and moist as they establish themselves.

planting in pots and containers

Lilies almost always do well in containers and gardeners new to growing lilies will often try them first in this way. Having grown bulbs of many types for well over 50 years, I am convinced that lilies are by far the easiest of any bulb to grow in pots and other containers. Potted bulbs are versatile: they can be given individual care and placed in a position to over-winter safely or they can be given some warmth under glass to encourage earlier blooming. Generally speaking, the bigger the pot the easier it is to grow good plants. A reasonably large amount of compost can be kept moist and at an even temperature much more easily than the quantity in a small pot. Pots are measured both by their diameter and their capacity, but the amount of compost they can hold is perhaps the more relevant measurement. I like to use earthenware pots where they are going to be seen, but use plastic ones just as readily. Plastic pots delay the drying out of the compost a little longer.

Apart from the considerations of space for the bulbs and the food supply from the compost, the pot size can be important for the stability of the whole, once the plants have grown. Three tall lilies, perhaps Trumpet kinds, can easily reach 1.2m (4ft) or even 2m (6ft) if planted early or grown for a second year in a pot. This tall growth can catch the wind and the container may be blown over if it is not securely weighed down. A large pot may not be completely stable but it will be less vulnerable than a smaller one.

POT SIZES

• A 2-litre pot (170mm/6⅔in diameter) would be the smallest practical size, which could serve for one normal Asiatic or three dwarf Asiatics. But the small size means that once the plants grow there can be problems preventing the compost from drying out and in a crowded pot it is difficult to manage proper watering from above.

• A 3-litre pot (190mm/7½in diameter) is the minimum size for a single bulb of a Trumpet or similar-sized lily and a reasonable size for three normal Asiatics – but this size may still be too small for many kinds of lily.

• A 5-litre pot (225mm/8¾in diameter) is good for three Asiatics or Orientals. It could house one large or three small Trumpets.

• A 7.5-litre pot (250mm/10in diameter) is considered a minimum size for three Trumpets or three large Orientals.

Half-tubs and other similarly generous containers are ideal for lilies provided they have adequate drainage holes. They were much favoured in the past when it was *de*

Oriental lilies such as 'Arena' need a lime-free soil but they can make fine container plants even in limy gardens.

rigueur to have crowded tubs of *L. regale* in any stately or other notable garden. Nowadays we have a much wider choice of lilies to grow in such containers, though the regal lily could still be many gardeners' first choice. Half-tubs have the advantage of being large enough to host a number of plants, creating a mini garden that can look colourful for months with and without lilies. Ideally such tubs or other large containers should be raised up a little way off the ground, whether it is on soil, gravel or paving. This will aid drainage, help prevent the incursion of slugs and snails, and lessen the chances of the container base rotting or deteriorating.

DISPLAYING LILIES IN POTS

A single lily in a pot can look splendid, but it cannot compare to the display of a trio growing together. Whenever possible, plant three bulbs per pot, and always of the same cultivar; try also to have matching sized bulbs so that the performance of all will be equal. Really large pots may be able to take more than three bulbs and give an even more sumptuous effect.

Most standard Asiatics grow to about 80cm (32in) tall and these will do well in pots without being too vulnerable to wind. Even taller kinds, such as Pink Perfection Group and other tall Trumpets, can be excellent in containers too, though it may be wise to add some supporting canes or twigs at the same time as potting the bulbs. Then, as the plants grow taller, it will be prudent to make sure the pot is well anchored. The bulbs will probably grow quite a lot taller if left in the same pot for a second year, especially if you scrape away the top layer of potting compost at the end of the first growing season and replace it with fresh.

COMPOSTS

Most Asiatics and Trumpets will cope with composts that contain a little lime, therefore it is permissible to use a John Innes potting compost, preferably No. 1 with only one dose of fertilizers. The advantages of the loam-based composts over those that are peat/humus-based ('general purpose' composts) are that they drain more freely, have more air in their structure and are easier to water if dryish. Humus-based composts can also be good, especially with plenty of grit added.

Composts marketed as 'ericaceous' will be free from lime and can safely be used for Oriental lilies as well as rhododendrons and similar lime-hating plants.

PLANTING LILIES IN CONTAINERS

1 Cover the drainage hole with a layer of broken crocks or pieces of polystyrene to prevent water and compost draining away.

2 Using a trowel, cover the bottom of the container with appropriate potting compost, then place the bulbs on this.

The addition of grit may make these composts easier to water, something that can be difficult if the compost is allowed to dry out. Dried-out pots are best lowered into a large vessel filled with water so that the water can then gradually work its way up through the compost by means of osmosis.

I do not think garden centres have yet started to offer composts specifically for lilies, though this could happen. Meanwhile, lily fanciers have independently formulated composts that seems to suit most lilies. Many feel that the plain John Innes compost is too free-draining and fast-drying to be completely practical but the addition of rotted organic matter helps it retain moisture, slightly acidifies the mix and makes it a little more root-friendly. I use a mix by volume of two parts John Innes No. 1 to one part rotted organic matter; other growers use a similar mix.

The use of peat is indefensible in many parts of the world on ecological grounds as commercial extraction has been destroying peat eco-systems. Now, however, more and more alternative sources of humus are being made available. Making your own leaf-mould by rotting down oak and beech leaves is another possible source. And properly made, well-matured material from the compost heap will be like manna from heaven to lilies.

3 Lay the bulbs on top of the compost, equally spaced and with their roots carefully spread out.

4 Cover the bulbs with more compost so they have a layer of at least 10cm (4in) over their noses (see page 132).

5 Leave a gap of at least 2.5cm (1in) at the top of the container. Water using a fine rose on a watering can or soak the compost by standing the pot in water.

POT PLANTING ROUTINE

Bulbs can be potted up at any time from the end of summer until late spring. Normally those planted early will do best, but the lily is a resilient pot plant and will respond to a little care if planted late. Pot-grown bulbs are best kept in a cool frost-free spot through the winter, preferably under cover if the weather is wet. The pots of growing lilies may be housed in an unheated greenhouse or cold frame but should be just as happy in the open if it is dry, as they enjoy a buoyant, airy atmosphere. A humid, close atmosphere may encourage fungus diseases such as botrytis. Keep aphids and other pests under control by an occasional spray.

Unless you wish to harvest the seed, cut off the flowerheads after blooming without removing any leaves. Continue to water the pots for six weeks or more to keep the bulbs healthy. Towards the end of summer, or in autumn, turn out the pots to reclaim the bulbs, together with any increase in the form of divisions of the bulb or bulbils clustering on the subterranean part of the stem. The foliage and stems of earlier-flowering lilies will have lost their vitality and may be turning brown, so they can be twisted away from the bulbs. Replant the bulbs, and perhaps grow the small ones on separately in pots or in the open ground. Make sure that they are all clearly labelled.

pests and diseases

THE LILY BEETLE

Lily beetles measure about 8mm (⅓in) long and almost half as wide. These pests are very visible, with their flat backs a brilliant orange-red.

The larvae are about the same length when fully grown but are hidden under a revolting mass of excreta. Under this dirty grey mass the creamy grubs steadily eat through the foliage.

PESTS

Lily bulbs are edible, as are the growing plants, and threats from larger pests come from rodents, rabbits and deer. Fences may have to be put in place to keep out deer and rabbits, which devour the emerging stems with relish. Our present garden was overrun with rabbits when we arrived, so I erected a wire-mesh fence just over 1m (3ft) above ground and more than 30cm (12in) below, with a short length at the base turned at right angles from the garden to deter excavating rabbits. Mice, voles and rats will find the bulbs a useful source of food, particularly in the winter, and for them cats and humane traps are recommended. The smaller pests affecting lilies include slugs, aphids, vine weevils and lily beetles.

Lily beetle The handsome lily beetle is the most annoying of the small pests and in parts of Europe its spread seems inexorable. These beetles usually appear in spring and can be active until autumn so it is vital to check plants carefully for their presence. While the adult beetle is conspicuous, the larvae hide under a mass of excreta that could well be blamed on passing birds. As both the adult beetles and the larvae live off the leaves of lilies, the result of a severe attack can be plants reduced to pathetic stems with a few threads where the foliage has gone.

As their presence is visible and their identification easily made, the beetle and its larvae can be collected by hand and destroyed. There is one hazard: often their reaction is to fall to the ground where they turn and lie on their backs, the bright red being replaced by black and almost impossible to see. It is best to lay a sheet of paper under the leaf being attacked before trying to pick off the beetle, so that the falling beast is captured. The second method of attack is to spray the foliage with a systemic insecticide, using a hand-held sprayer or a ready-made pressurized can. The beetle and larvae eat their leaf and ingest some of the poison, which usually kills the larvae quickly. The beetle may be a little more resistant but it moves more sluggishly and can easily be gathered up.

A regular inspection of the plants will ensure that any invasion is spotted early enough to be dealt with. It is only if the pests are left undisturbed that plants are severely attacked. In my experience the most active season for the beetles is in late spring, the time that coincides with the maximum growth rate of the plants and before their flowers start opening.

Lesser pests Slugs and snails can attack lily bulbs and the young stems. They are usually at their most active in early spring, at a time when lily shoots can be emerging from the bulb and breaking the soil surface. A stem can be weakened by nibbling slugs and the whole plant jeopardized. Clean cultivation of the soil will help reduce the slug population, traditional traps can take a useful toll and pellets

The pale striations on the foliage indicate that this lily is suffering from cucumber mosaic virus. If the plant is not destroyed, the virus can be passed to other healthy plants — most efficiently by aphids.

strategically positioned will deal with others. It is now possible to purchase pellets that are harmless to pets and birds; the dead slugs collected by birds are harmless.

Aphids may attack the growing lily plant, especially the clustered flower buds. These will be killed by systemic or other insecticides. It is best to attack in good time before they have started to damage the tissue of the flowers and cause them to open distorted. The other reason to keep on top of aphids is that as they suck juice from the lilies they may transmit virus they have picked up from infected plants elsewhere. The injection of these viruses will not be immediately evident but the following year could result in a lot of plants having to be destroyed.

Vine weevils can be a nuisance. The adult is a grey-black insect with brown flecks, about 9mm (⅜in) long, recognized by ridged lines running longitudinally. It feeds on foliage. The plump, creamy-white grubs are more dangerous, as they feed on roots and can leave a plant without the means to support itself. An apparently healthy plant may suddenly wilt, and when the roots are examined grubs will be found. The vine weevil is not normally a major threat to lilies, but grubs can attack potted bulbs. There are a number of effective chemical treatments.

DISEASES

Virus Of a number of viruses that can attack lilies, by far the most common is the cucumber mosaic virus which, despite its name, is found in a wide range of plants. The symptoms are paler patterns of stripes on the foliage. When well established this virus may cause distortion of leaves and flowers and a brittle texture to both. Tulip breaking virus causes a mottled effect on the foliage. Lily symptomless virus is an unusual one that may be suspected if for no reason a plant or group of lilies appears to lose its vitality and look debilitated. This is not widespread at present, so check other possible causes for deterioration of plants before destroying them.

There is no cure for virus so all attacked bulbs should be destroyed before insects spread it further. It is possible to pass on the trouble if a knife used for cutting an infected stem is then used on a clean plant.

Fungus The widespread *Botrytis elliptica* can cause severe damage when conditions are favourable. It spreads quickly in wet, airless conditions, so humid weather will foster this disease. If lilies are crowded together in places where air movement is restricted the fungus can attack. It will usually start by turning lower leaves brown, which at first may look like blotches caused by frost. The leaves become limp and wither and a major attack could leave a whole stem defoliated. Though this looks unsightly and plants are indeed weakened, they are rarely completely killed. Keep the disease at bay by ensuring plenty of air around your lilies. Spraying with Bordeaux mixture early in the growing season can help control botrytis but it is not a cure.

For many, propagation is the heart of gardening and for them the lily is the ideal hobby plant. It has many successful means of increase. Seed is obviously nature's first choice and in the wild this is how lilies maintain their presence. Gardeners may follow suit or decide to exploit the plant's natural bulb division in some way – something that is likely to happen more freely under the benign conditions of cultivation than in the wild. Bulblets form on the underground part of the stem of many kinds of lily, while bulbils may appear in the leaf axils of some. But the most

growing lilies: propagating

popular method is the ability of scales broken from the bulb to form small bulbs along their fractured edges.

There is a fundamental difference between seed raising and all other methods of propagation, which are vegetative, and both have advantages. The advantages of vegetative propagation are considerable. First, all new plants will have identical genetic material to the parent bulbs and, being parts of a single clone, will be able to produce a uniform performance. (The definition of 'clone' is plants with identical DNA, so separate plants of a clone are effectively divided parts of one individual.) Flowers will be the same, as will blooming time, plant height and habit. Vegetative propagation is normally also much easier than by seed as it takes less care than the successful germination and growing on of small seedlings.

Self-pollinated seed from species will broadly reproduce the characteristics of the parents, but there will be some variation, perhaps small but possibly significant. A little change in flower colour is easily noticed; very often orange species also have yellow forms due to a lesser concentration of the colour pigment carotene. Less obvious may be a tendency to bloom a little later or earlier than the norm. Optimum height of the plants is another variable that will be ascertained only after a period. It is always worth renewing stock of species by seed, not only to take advantage of a possible beneficial variation but more importantly to introduce new stock that is free from virus and other diseases.

Virus can be insidious in the way it reduces the overall efficiency of plants. Sometimes this is a rapid process and with obvious symptoms, but the attack may affect the lilies' vitality only slowly, with initially very faint signs. The most worrying factor is that while the effect of virus will be minimal on one lily, if aphids transfer the virus to others the result of infection on the new host can be catastrophic. There is no cure for virus within the usual abilities of an amateur grower, which means that any infected plant reproduced vegetatively will pass the virus to all propagated plants. Obviously the choice of healthy bulbs for propagation is vital.

natural bulb division

Dig at some distance from a stem as it may not have grown directly upright from the bulb.

The concentric bulb has two noses and is ready to divide, while a new small bulb has been easily detached.

There is huge diversity in the bulbs' natural rates of increase, varying from slowly dividing ones to others with rabbit-like fecundity. Increase rates will depend on the type of bulb, but also on soil and environmental factors. The concentric bulbs of Asiatic hybrids normally split regularly, a reasonably sized bulb easily dividing after a season's growth into two or three bulbs of similar size to the original when planted. LA hybrids can considerably outstrip this performance. Trumpets and Aurelians tend to expand their bulb size before dividing but often develop new, smaller bulbs as side shoots around the base of the bulb or within the outer ring of scales.

After a bulb blooms, the flowering stem dies down and divides the basal plate of the original bulb into two. Depending on the vigour of the plant and its age, this division will be more or less apparent. In time, the tissue between the two parts will perish and two bulbs will function independently. Often, however, growers will seize the opportunity to split the dividing bulbs in autumn, some eight weeks after flowering. They crack open the divide by hand or plunge a knife down through the hole made where the defunct flower stem has twisted away.

Rhizomatous bulbs growing under good garden conditions can engender at least two new growing points from each original one. After a couple of seasons the whole rootstock can be divided using a knife, so that each new piece has a section of the old rhizome and at least one new growing point, distinguished by its paler scales. This can normally be done towards the end of summer.

The natural division of bulbs can cause overcrowded clusters in just a few seasons in garden conditions. The greater the competition between them, the less likely they are to grow into the fat high-performers we desire. It therefore makes sense to lift and divide bulbs regularly, perhaps after one, two or three seasons.

LIFTING BULBS

The time to lift bulbs is usually six weeks or so after blooming has ended, which means that most Asiatics can be dug in late summer. The tops may have been partially cut back to dispense with the dead flowerheads (unless seed is to be collected) and the foliage, if not obviously faded or failing, will not be working efficiently, so the stems can be sacrificed and the bulbs shaken free of soil. There may well be a number of bulblets clasping the stem (see opposite).

Lifting bulbs is an opportunity to remove slugs and to cut away or tidy up any damaged scales. Cut surfaces should be treated with fungicide. The roots are almost useless, so loose ones can be removed, but the stronger ones can be useful to anchor the bulbs into their new homes. These bulbs will soon begin to make a new root system, which is the beginning of their annual growth cycle. Sometimes the new bulbs are dividing into two or more independent bulbs. These are easily prised apart by thrusting a knife-point down the flower-stem hole into the basal

This raised bulb has several below-ground bulblets still attached to the stem.

The same bulb with the stem bulblets detached and all ready for planting.

plate. It is a matter of choice whether you do this or replant any multi-nosed bulbs as one. Bulbs are not meant to be out of the ground for any length of time, so you should replant them in the border or in pots immediately. If you cannot do this straight away, store them in a container and cover them with peat or similar material that is damp rather than wet and place in a cool spot. Store the bulbs for no longer than is necessary. The aim is to encourage them to make a fresh extensive root system well before the onset of winter weather.

The Trumpets, Aurelians, many Orientals and Orienpets are likely to bloom later than Asiatics so a six-week period after blooming brings them closer to winter. But there should still be time to dig, divide and replant so that the bulbs can re-establish themselves with strong root systems. If at lifting time the plants still look green and active, cut the stems to half their length and keep attached to the bulbs. The shortened stems will return goodness to the bulbs and make useful handles when replanting. They also serve to mark the bulbs' positions in their new homes.

BELOW-GROUND STEM BULBLETS

Many lilies are dynamic procreators. A majority have at least some potential to produce bulblets on the portion of stem in the soil. The Asiatic group of species and all the Asiatic hybrids are particularly energetic in these endeavours, especially if the plants are growing vigorously. It is not unusual to see bulblet tips jostling together and pushing through the soil surface next to the stem. Their number and size can vary widely, from one to ten. LA hybrids can be extraordinarily prolific and may have bulblets as large as golf balls. Most others will be around the size of children's marbles, ranging down to minute ones not normally worth bothering with.

The six- to eight-week period after flowering can be an important time for these bulblets to fatten up ready for harvesting, usually when the main bulbs are lifted. Like the mother bulbs, they are best planted immediately; some will have already developed roots. If you plant them between the replanted main bulbs, one advantage is that the name of the plant is known, and another is that the cloned youngsters are in the same care regime as the parents, which will suit them as well. A possible disadvantage is that young plants could be swamped by the larger ones. If you do not want non-flowering young plants among your full-sized specimens, carefully label the bulblets and grow them on for a season in pots or nursery rows in a spare part of the garden. Most reasonably sized bulblets of Asiatics should have grown to flowering size after one growing season.

Martagon types can produce bulblets but are not noted for it. Trumpets will be less generous than Asiatics, though plants with Aurelian blood may be a little more free. Of the normal producers, stems that have had their potential flowering heads removed in infancy will often give more and larger bulblets.

LEAF-AXIL BULBILS

Lily species that produce bulbils in their leaf axils can be very generous, especially the tiger lily (*L. lancifolium*), the European *L. bulbiferum* and a rare Asiatic Trumpet, *L. sargentiae*. *L. bulbiferum* has forms and clones that do not normally produce bulbils, including the best-known, *L. bulbiferum* var. *croceum*. Asiatic hybrids often have the potential to grow bulbils too and some will do this spontaneously, while others can be encouraged to perform by cutting off the flowerhead as soon as you see the small green flower buds developing. Often young, non-flowering bulbs will produce stems with a good number of bulbils.

The tiger lily bulbils are a dark purple where they receive sunlight and each leaf axil may support one, two or even three. As the stems are very leafy, each plant can have up to a hundred bulbils per stem. In the natural course of events these fall off as they ripen in the autumn, by which stage they may already have started to grow roots and sometimes have a small leaf. The fallen bulbils plunge roots into the soil which pull the bulbils down, contracting concertina-like to effect this.

Bulbils can be harvested as they develop, from the end of summer to autumn. The fat ripe ones snap off easily and younger ones can be left on for collection later. Plant them in drills in an open garden, as you might deal with vegetable seeds, or in pots or trays using a humus-rich but open, gritty compost. Planted early, they will root readily and produce leaves so that plants are established before winter, when they will lose their foliage and mark time until spring. Planted out in spring, they should grow strongly through the year, with most flowering the following summer.

CLONING FROM SCALES

This is a favourite bit of magic. It can be done at any time of the year but the easiest period will be in very early spring so that the resulting young plants can be grown on strongly through the growing year. Detach the scales and put them in a growing medium, either vermiculite or gritty compost (see opposite). Once the scales have produced embryo bulbs along their fractured edges, they can be potted up in pots or trays. Grow them on until each bulb has produced two or three leaves, at which stage the plants are probably ready to plant out in the open. If, when the scales are examined after the six- to eight-week gestation period, the bulbs look very small, they can be closed up again in their bags and given longer to fatten up.

In warm parts of the world where well-drained soils can be kept moist, scales can be detached and grown on outdoors in drills. Some bulbs, like the Martagons, have very brittle scales and it is almost impossible to lift or handle them without some becoming detached. Left in the soil, these will form small bulbs without any leaves for the first year and will then increase in size over the seasons until they reach flowering size – a period that can be five years or longer.

CLONING FROM SCALES

1 Select a healthy bulb and break off scales close to the basal plate. With overlapping scales, it is easiest to work around the bulb until enough scales are detached. If it is a precious small bulb you may have to be content with one or two, but a large bulb may yield six large scales without being drastically weakened. Discard slug-attacked, damaged or apparently diseased scales.

2 Soak the scales in a systemic fungicide according to the maker's instructions but usually for 15–20 minutes. Give each group of scales a clearly written, indelible label.

3 There is now a choice. You can enclose the scales in a plastic bag with a handful or two of moistened, clean vermiculite or similar inert material. Allow it to take up as much water as it can for 5 minutes, then drain before use. Close the bag, with plenty of air inside, and label it. Place each bag in a safe place (not necessarily in the dark) and keep at 17–21°C (65–70°F).

4 Alternatively, after soaking the scales in fungicide, insert them into a tray of gritty compost with only the tip of each scale exposed. Label the tray, then soak it from below and allow to drain.

5 Enclose the tray in a plastic bag and seal to maintain a moist atmosphere. After 6–8 weeks, open the bag and prise up a scale or two to examine. They should have one to five embryo bulbs along their fractured bases. Each will have begun producing roots and possibly the first small leaf.

6 Introduce the little bulbs into gritty, humus-rich compost in pots or trays. Plant a whole scale, with the bulbs 2.5cm (1in) below the surface, or detach the bulbs and plant separately. Grow on until each has produced 2–3 leaves, when the plants will be ready to pot on or plant out in the open.

raising lilies from seeds

Late-ripening seedpods have been brought under cover in autumn to continue ripening. Place a sheet of paper below the pods to catch any falling seed.

There are a number of benefits to growing from seed. First, you can be sure that the plants are initially free from virus and other diseases. Among lily species there are some that are only available from seed. As a pod can easily contain 50–100 viable seeds, there is scope for a population explosion. There is always a chance of some variation within a species, so gardeners can play the evolutionary game and ensure 'the survival of the fittest' as he or she envisages it. Of course, hybrid seed can produce huge variations from a single pod of a self-fertilized cultivar. Controlled crosses stand a chance of combining the qualities that the breeder has in mind, but betting on the outcome is hazardous. There are lots of surprises, but while there are swans galore, ugly ducklings are extraordinarily rare.

There is normally a six- to eight-week period between successful pollination (see page 150) and seed ripening. The later the flowering season, the slower the seed ripens. Sometimes the late-ripening pods have to be cut and brought inside to be finished off, once it has become too wet and cold outdoors. Hang the cut stems upside down in a dry, airy, warm spot such as a conservatory or greenhouse. Lay sheets of newspaper below the stems to catch any seed that is released. Moisture is a particular danger to late-ripening pods as fungus can attack them and its mycelium grows quickly through the pods, destroying the seed as it goes.

When the seedpods ripen, the tops crack open and the disc-like seed can be blown away. If you are going to be away from the garden at this time it would be prudent to enclose the pods in muslin, held by elastic bands. The dry seed can be shelled out from the pods and the chaff lightly blown away. While chaff is without definition, viable seed is fatter. If a light is shone through the seed, the embryo can be clearly seen. It is a matter of nice judgement how strongly you blow to remove the chaff without losing lively seed, but it is not that difficult.

SOWING THE SEED

Seed needs moisture, warmth and air to germinate and this is usually provided by seed compost in a pot or tray. Damp vermiculite in a sealed bag or glass jar would also serve and seed will even germinate on damp kitchen paper in a sealed plastic bag. Neither the vermiculite nor the paper provides any nourishment, so the germinated seedlings will have to be transferred to a suitable growing medium – a gritty, ericaceous compost – when the reserves from the seed run out. However, it is more usual to sow directly into such a compost mix.

These flat, disc-like seeds are from a Trumpet lily, which produces larger seed than some smaller species and hybrids.

Seed can be sown immediately after harvesting or saved and dealt with at the end of winter or the very beginning of spring. Early-ripened seed sown in late summer can germinate immediately to produce small bulbs and leaves before winter. These are best grown under glass in an airy atmosphere and sprayed with fungicide, otherwise fungus may cause damping-off and perhaps kill the tiny plants. The argument that as Nature sows immediately this might be the course to follow is fairly compelling. Normally the safest place for seed is in the soil.

On the other hand, if seed is stored safely and sown in very early spring, the germinating seed and young plants will have the benefit of improving weather conditions which should encourage steady, rapid growth without any of the checks that winter might conjure up. Good seed storage means enclosing the clean, dry seed with air in a sealed packet and keeping it cool, for example in a domestic refrigerator (not a deep-freeze compartment).

GERMINATION

Seed germinates in several different ways, depending on the type of lily. Some begins to grow by sending out a shoot that develops a swelling at the end that is the beginning of the bulb. The shoot curves, humps up to form a loop which breaks through the soil surface and then pulls up its own free end to form a narrow strap-like 'cotyledon' leaf, often with the seed case still attached at the end and waving aloft like a little flag. As the bulb grows it gathers enough strength to send up its first true leaf, a spear-shaped one. This starting method is known as 'epigeal' or 'above-ground' germination.

The alternative behaviour is called 'hypogeal' or 'below-ground' germination. These seeds produce a shoot that tends to descend – perhaps 2.5cm (1in) or so – and forms a tiny bulb, usually below the seed case. The food reserves stored in the seed are used to make the shoot and the beginnings of the little bulb with its first roots. When the roots start gathering nourishment, the bulb sends up its first leaf, a true spear-shaped one and not a cotyledon; this is the first sign of successful germination. With some kinds of lily this single leaf is the total foliage for the duration of the first year.

Both epigeal and hypogeal methods are further divided into those that germinate immediately, that is within four to seven weeks, and those that delay matters, perhaps for a few months. Thus we have four germinating categories (see the introduction to each species group in Choosing Species, page 40): epigeal immediate, epigeal delayed, hypogeal immediate and hypogeal delayed. By far the largest categories are the epigeal immediate and the hypogeal delayed. Many gardeners will be sowing more of the epigeal immediate types than of any others and luckily these are the most straightforward.

The way we manage our seed can depend on its germination method. In the absence of any other advice, seeds are best sown as soon after harvest or purchase as possible, since seed that is not properly stored will begin to lose its vitality.

SOWING TIMES FOR ALL CATEGORIES

Epigeal immediate and hypogeal immediate Seed harvested early may be sown straight away and should provide small bulbs before winter. Seed saved in autumn or later is best kept dry and cool until the end of winter, then sown. Give each seed about 6cm^2 (1sq in) of space and keep moist rather than wet. Use a fungicide spray early on. Seed sown in spring should start growing quickly and produce progressively more leaves, making a rosette of these before attempting to produce a stem (this usually happens in the second season). When leaves start to turn yellow in autumn, the bulbs of vigorous kinds can be 2.5cm (1in) or more in diameter. The aim is to grow a bulb large enough to plant out in a nursery row or permanent flowering position by autumn. Slower growers can be kept just moist in pots over winter and grown on for a further year before planting out.

Really strong kinds such as *L. regale* can be sown outside in early spring in temperate parts of the world and some bulbs may be big enough to have a flower in their second year if grown well.

Epigeal delayed Sow seed straight from the pods or keep until the end of winter. Some batches may germinate together but others may start into growth at intervals. You can abandon the nursery pots when sufficient plants have emerged and been pricked out.

Hypogeal delayed The main types that behave in this way are the Orientals and the Martagons. The seeds need an initial 12-week period of relative warmth, say 21°C (70°F), during which time they will form tiny bulbs. These then need six weeks of cool conditions, preferably just above freezing, to break the bulbs' dormancy and trigger the formation of the first leaves. Seeds sown in the autumn and kept warm will therefore be ready for their cool period by the end of winter and should be producing leaves at the beginning of spring. The plants should then grow away through spring and summer.

L. martagon, with its relatives and hybrids, ripens seed early. If this is sown after harvesting it will receive the warm period naturally, followed by the cool of winter, and will then be ready to display its first leaves in spring. The seed of Martagons is usually plentiful; it can be sown in weed-free cultivated soil in the open. Even if a proportion of the seed is lost to natural hazards, there will still be plenty of survivors.

1 Sow seed in pots at the end of winter using a compost made up of topsoil or loam – or humus-based compost mixed with equal parts grit or washed coarse sand. Commercial composts may be safest. Fill the pots to within 2.5cm (1in) of the top, then sow the seed at roughly 1cm (½in) intervals and cover with at least a 1cm (½in) layer of grit.

2 Soak the pots in water, then drain and enclose in a plastic bag or plunge them up to their rims in the soil in a bed or border outside and cover with plastic or glass. Fast-germinating seed ('immediate') will show through in 4–7 weeks, while delayed kinds may not appear until the following year.

3 Grow the seedlings on for a year or two within the nursery pot or until they form a stem. Plant out in early spring or early autumn into well-drained soil and keep moist during dry periods up to the end of autumn. It is not exceptional to have the first flowers from *L. amabile, L. pumilum, L. regale, L. formosanum* and *L. longiflorum* in their second season.

Seed of Orientals can be late ripening and may be sown in pots at the beginning of winter, as already suggested. Alternatively, find some clean jars with screw-cap tops to use as incubators. Moisten some vermiculite with clean water, then drain away the surplus before placing a handful or two inside the jar. Soak seed of Orientals overnight in clean water to wash away any natural germination inhibitors. Place the seed and a label in the container. Shake it, with the top secured, and stick a further label on the outside. Make sure some of the seed is at the edge of the jar so that its progress can be observed after placing the containers in a warmish spot at around 21°C (70°F).

After about three months, small bulbs will be seen. When these are fully formed and beginning to produce roots, you can remove them and pot them up into a gritty ericaceous compost. Place the pots in a cool spot in the open, or in a cold frame or unheated greenhouse. When leaves appear, give the pots a touch more warmth and keep them reasonably moist. Alternatively, give the little bulbs in their glass containers their cool period *in situ*. Once stimulated into root and leaf growth, prick out the young bulbs when there is a leaf big enough to handle.

breeding new lilies

This is something that anyone can do successfully – the process is simple and the rewards great. As the professional breeders have their eyes firmly fixed on the value of good cut flowers, it must be hoped that some of the rejects of their breeding programmes – kinds with outward-facing or pendent flowers – can be passed into the garden bulb trade. It is with flowers of such habits that amateur breeders could do stalwart work. Even if new seedlings never get beyond the garden fence, the pleasure to be obtained from raising new kinds is very special. Fortunately it is almost impossible to raise an ugly lily.

Cultivars will often have a complicated heredity and self-pollinated seed may give rise to seedlings none of which looks much like the mother, but there will be features that are similar even if they are only leaf form, height and flowering period. The gardener may view cultivars and think how one could be improved in certain respects by the input of genetic material from another. Cross-pollination may give the desired effect or may produce surprises with new combinations of features.

THE TECHNIQUE

Lily anthers usually produce large quantities of pollen, so these should be removed to prevent self-pollination (see opposite). The stigmas become sticky when they are at their most receptive – usually a day or so after the flower has opened – so this is the time to carry out hand pollination. If the chosen parents are not blooming at the same time, you can save pollen from the earlier flower for later use. Remove anthers before the pollen has been lost and store them in clean plastic tubes such as film canisters or those used for medicinal tablets. If the anthers are fresh they will be damp, so leave the containers open until the anthers have fully dried. Then seal them and store in a refrigerator, carefully labelled. Pollen will keep for weeks or even months in such conditions.

Once pollinated, label the flower or flowers with clearly written labels. It is usual to write the name of the seed parent first, so that a label might read 'Sorbet x Lollipop' where 'Sorbet' is the seed parent whose stigmas have received the 'Lollipop' pollen. While most pollination can take place in the garden, bulbs may be potted up and the crossing conducted under glass. An advantage is that the flowers will come earlier and any resulting seed will ripen much sooner. The warmer, more humid conditions may also help to facilitate fertilization.

The laws of inheritance obtain in the lily family and experience will give some guide as to the likely outcomes of a breeding exercise. In the simplest case, a characteristic will be governed by a single gene with two forms (alleles). Spots on the flowers could be governed by such a gene, one form favouring spotted flowers and the other spotless ones. An Asiatic lily inheriting genes from both parents favouring spots will obviously have spotted offspring. If a pair of spotless genes is

POLLINATING LILIES BY HAND

To prevent self-pollination, remove the anthers by hand or by using tweezers, preferably before they have split and begun to release their pollen.

Dust the prominent stigma all over with the foreign pollen, either by dragging an anther of the pollen parent over the stigma surface or by transferring some pollen to it using a small watercolour brush.

inherited, the flower will be spot-free. But if a plant inherits both gene forms, the flowers will be spotted because in this case the one favouring spots is 'dominant', while the spotless is 'recessive'. A spotted individual carrying a recessive gene for the spotless state will pass this on through half its egg cells and half its pollen grains. If this individual is self-fertilized, the recessive effect will only be revealed if one recessive gene links up with a similar one – a one in four chance.

BREEDING PLANS

Even in the smallest-scale breeding operation it pays to have a clear idea of your aims. As a single pod can contain 50–100 seeds, it is important to show discretion. New possibilities will tempt further experimentation each season, so that you may soon have a large number of plants at various stages. Some kinds will take longer than others to reach flowering-sized bulbs. Asiatics sown in late winter and well grown may have their first blooms in midsummer the following year, while some Trumpets may bloom after two years' growth.

There are endless possibilities for small-scale raisers. LAs and Asiatics that face out or down are relatively scarce and may be thought more graceful than the numerous upward kinds. And while most Asiatics are without scent, a few are gently perfumed; gardeners would enjoy a series of scented novelties.

Consider the use of species lilies such as *L. pumilum* to provide dainty, many-headed spikes of flowers. *L. amabile* and its yellow form *L. amabile* var. *luteum*, together with the small *L. concolor*, may be used to add brilliance to the surface sheen of petals. These are species with good lime-tolerance and disease resistance to impart to seedlings. There is still something to be gained by using *L. bulbiferum* with its very early-flowering habit and indifference to lime, while *L. dauricum* and *L. wilsonii* have distinctive flowers and are easily crossed with a wide range of mates, the first imparting a robust constitution and often early blooms to seedlings. Pendent flowers may be bred from such species as *L. pumilum*, *L. davidii* and *L. lancifolium*.

Gardeners can never get enough of the Martagon-type hybrids and this is just the field where the amateur could surge ahead. The use of the unusual tangerine *L. tsingtauense* with upward-facing flowers and polished surfaces could widen the range of possibilities among the Martagons.

appendix

classification of lily species

Comber's widely respected classification of 1949 gives us seven groups: Martagon, North American, Candidum, Oriental, Asian, Trumpet and Dauricum. The Martagons are seen as the most primitive types, the closest to the prototype *Lilium*, followed by the North Americans. The classification is based on various factors listed in order of their adjudged importance.

Germination
(a) hypogeal (above-ground)
(b) epigeal (below-ground)
(a) delayed – after some months (b) immediate – after four to seven weeks

Leaf arrangement
(a) whorled, i.e. rings of leaves at the same level (b) scattered

Bulb scales
(a) jointed (b) entire

Seed weight
(a) heavy (b) light

Bulb shape and habit
(a) erect (b) sub-rhizomatous
(c) rhizomatous
(d) stoloniferous

Petals
(a) papillose – with raised points (b) smooth

Nectary
(a) pubescent, i.e. with soft hairs
(b) glabrous, ie. hairless

Flower form
(a) turk's cap (b) trumpet

Bulb colour
(a) white (b) purple

Stem habit
(a) erect (b) stoloniform

Leaf stalks
(a) petiole, i.e. obvious stalk
(b) obscure or none

Stigma
(a) large (b) small

Stem roots
(a) present (b) absent

Stems per bulb
(a) one (b) sometimes more

further species
to those described in the main text (pages 42–67)

OTHER MARTAGON SPECIES (Group 1)

L. distichum This species from central Korea, north-east China and neighbouring territories grows in woodland soils in cool conditions. It has a few horizontal or slightly downward-tilted flowers on stems that can reach an exceptional 1m (3ft), but are more often half this. Well-endowed stems can have a dozen blooms. Foliage is confined to a single whorl with perhaps a few scattered leaves above. Narrow petals spread outwards before recurving only at the tips. Their colour is tangerine to pale red, maybe with a few beauty spots.

L. medeoloides Also from Korea and surrounding countries, this species is very obviously a Martagon type, but this is the mini version with stems having only one whorl of leaves and normally under 60cm (2ft) in stature. Pendent flowers have petals curved back but not so extremely as the team leader and their colour is a rich tangerine with dark spots; there are red forms too. It needs an open, humus-rich soil.

OTHER N. AMERICAN SPECIES (Group 2)

Group 2a
L. bolanderi From 45cm (18in) to1.2m (4ft), the slender wiry stems carry a few flowers of an unusual deep burgundy-red in the best forms, and there are others of a rather muddier orange-red. Funnel-shaped blooms are held horizontally or slightly downwards with petal tips just recurving.
L. columbianum This is a widely distributed species usually growing to around 1m (3ft) high, with medium-sized bright orange flowers spotted maroon. Colours can vary, with some all-red ones. Usually generous with nodding flowers. Relatively easy to grow from seed but not necessarily long-lived.

L. humboldtii This resembles the tiger lily but with orthodox N. American whorled leaves. Nodding turk's caps are golden orange, heavily spotted maroon except at the tips, the spots sometimes being ringed in gold. This is a stronger species than many and capable of 30 or more flowers to a good stem.

L. rubescens Rare and like *L. washingtonianum* but with the bells swung upright. Half of each petal forms the bell, the other half points out to make a star shape. It usually opens white but becomes flushed with pinky mauve in its prime, then turns a senescent purple before dying off. A light peppering with purple in the base is an optional extra that in some forms is taken almost to excess and invades the whole flower. There are no golden rules for success but a start should be made with very good drainage and an open-structured soil.

L. washingtonianum Rare in cultivation, this has horizontally held white trumpet blooms dotted with the purple that may also be staining the base.

Group 2b
L. maritimum Another coastal species from further south than *L. occidentale* (see below). Red-orange spotted flowers are fairly gently recurved.

L. nevadense Found inland in California and Nevada, this species looks like a half-sized relative of *L. pardalinum* but it has a scent.

L. occidentale This grows in a strip of land along the Pacific coast of north California and south Oregon, where it is under threat from increasing human activity. Bulbs make their home on hummocks of soil that protrude from wet, boggy areas. Nodding red flowers with orange and green bases have much-recurved petals. Height 60cm–1.5m (2–5ft).

L. parryi Rather lightweight whorls of foliage as well as scattered leaves clothe wiry stems 75cm–1.5m (2ft 6in–5ft) high, carrying ten or more wide golden bell-trumpet flowers usually without any hint of orange. I have counted 80 on an exceptionally crowded stem.

L. parvum This species grows in the hills behind the distribution of *L. occidentale* and *L. maritimum*. Small horizontal bells are usually a rich orange that gives way to gold and a green centre. Bell-shaped blooms hang as buds, then swing up to the horizontal as they open. There are 12–25 flowers to a stem 1.2–1.8m (4–6ft) tall.

L. vollmeri A *pardalinum*-type plant built on more slender lines, the stems being some 60–90cm (2–3ft) high, well furnished with whorls of slender leaves. Six or more typical turk's caps are vivid tangerine dotted maroon-red but with golden throats. Formerly listed as *L. roezlii*.

L. wigginsii Hailing from the wooded mountainsides of Oregon and California, this is a pleasing plant that is not impossible in the garden although it is not necessarily a dangerous land-grabber. It has upright leaves on dark green stems 60cm–1.5m (2–5ft) tall. A pyramid of nodding amber flowers may number 10–25, with tiny purple spots overall. Petals and leaves are slender, giving the whole plant a daintier feel than some. Needs cool, humus-rich soil.

Group 2c
L. carolinianum (syn. *L. michauxii*) This is rarely seen in cultivation, neither bulbs nor seeds are readily available. The species grows in dry, well-drained soils in the south-eastern states of the USA. Stoloniferous bulbs produce stems 30cm–1m (1–3ft) high, with whorls of relatively broad lanceolate leaves waved at the margins. One to five hanging, scented flowers are of typical *pardalinum* form and shine in shades of orange-red but with pale yellow throats. It is a stem rooter that prefers lime-free soil of humus-enriched sand.

L. iridollae This is a very rarely grown species with tiny bulbs and small golden flowers with much recurved petals. It is unusual in producing a cluster of narrow basal leaves after blooming and keeping these through the winter in the manner of *L. candidum*. It grows 45cm–1.2m (18in–4ft) tall.

L. michiganense A widespread species with showy, waxy, orange-red flowers heavily spotted on the lower two-thirds of the petals. Like *L. canadense*, it has long sloping pedicels, and just at the end these turn down to have the blooms in a fully pendent pose. They start with a funnel shape before recurving sharply. There may be three to seven stems, 1.2–1.5m (4–5ft) tall, on an established plant but exceptional ones will number a few dozen. Like its relatives, the stoloniferous bulbs enjoy a deep humus-rich soil; it is reported to be lime-tolerant.

Group 2d

L. catesbaei A tiny little tuft of a bulb supports a mini stem of 22–45cm (9–18in), with leaves arranged alternately and more or less clasping the stem. An upward-facing flower is relatively large, with petals having narrow hafts so that you can see through the flower; the petals spread and recurve gently at the tips. This is an awkward plant that produces a tiny rosette of narrow leaves in the autumn to be cared for through the winter; not a likely garden plant.

L. philadelphicum A small, dainty wild flower that is only fleetingly known in cultivation. Stems grow 45cm–1m (18in–3ft) tall, with whorled foliage and scattered leaves. The upward-facing flowers are red-orange, spotted golden at the base; the petals point outwards from these goblet bases.

OTHER CANDIDUM SPECIES (Group 3)

Group 3b

L. carniolicum An alpine species with chunky turk's cap flowers

of rusty red. Half a dozen flowers can be held by a 45cm–1m (18in–3ft) stem, the scattered leaves being a little hairy along their margins and the veins on the lower side. *L. carniolicum albanicum*, a smaller plant with lemon or golden flowers, has been given specific, sub-specific and varietal status at different times; perhaps it is simplest to regard it as a variety. *L. carniolicum jankae* is another variation, but with yellow or orange flowers.

L. ciliatum Once confused with *L. pyrenaicum* and other species, this plant hails from northern Turkey. Large bulbs produce stems 60cm–1.5m (2–5ft) tall, clothed with long, narrow leaves that are rough to the touch and margined with hairs. Flowers are ivory or primrose-yellow, but with a purplish centre and a light spray of tiny dots. The hanging flowers have recurving petals but the shape is wider than the restricted turk's caps of *L. pyrenaicum*. This is an interesting species, without any special garden merit beyond that of others.

L. pomponium A pleasing species from the Maritime Alps, with stems 30–75cm (1ft–2ft 6in) tall, with generous amounts of grassy, narrow leaves and dainty heads of one to ten smallish nodding turk's caps. These are firm textured, lightly peppered with tiny dots and bright red-orange but without the lacquer finish of *L. chalcedonicum*.

Group 3c

L. polyphyllum A species from the Himalayas that seems ill-equipped for cultivation since it dislikes wet winters. Reports of stems 2.1m (7ft) high with up to 30 flowers certainly whet the appetite, though more normal

endeavours are around 1.2m (4ft), with six flowers. Hanging blooms are ivory-white outside but creamy inside with a more or less mauve blush and lengthwise streaks of mauve-purple. The petals make a funnel before opening out and perhaps recurving a little.

OTHER ORIENTAL SPECIES (Group 4)

Group 4c

L. japonicum A lovely wide pink trumpet species that is likely to do better in New Zealand, parts of Australia and Oregon than in Britain. The wiry stems have slender, dark leaves and usually carry one to three heavily perfumed flowers, held horizontally.

L. nobilissimum This is a white trumpet species from one of the southern Japanese islands. Flowers are 10cm (4in) across and deep, their pure white being enhanced by a green exterior and golden anthers. It can have up to six perfumed blooms to a stem 75cm–1.2m (2ft 6in–4ft) high. In temperate climates this is likely to be a greenhouse plant.

Group 4d

L. brownii This looks like the traditional white trumpet lily, and rather a special one at that, but it is in fact an Oriental with *L. speciosum* and *L. auratum* as its disparate relatives. Its 1–1.2m (3–4ft) sloping stems are well-clothed with narrow leaves and above these come the very large, dark mahogany buds. The open flowers are sparkling white with golden throats and chocolate anthers that soon become golden with pollen. There are forms with paler pinkish buds, rather than chocolate. The form *L. brownii* var. *australe* is usually the most

vigorous and can double the standard height. Its buds may be greenish, its flowers are as large or larger than the species, while the foliage may be even narrower. I have enjoyed periods of success with this species, alas all too short. The bulbs, composed of many narrow scales, seem to be quite vigorous for a while, then unaccountably fail – but perhaps others will be luckier.

OTHER ASIAN SPECIES (Group 5)

Group 5a

L. papilliferum A rare species in cultivation, a smallish plant that might suggest one of the dark forms of *L. martagon* in its flowers, though the leaves are scattered. It grows some 45cm (18in) high in normal circumstances, but is able to double this. Petals are tightly curled back, the colour a deep maroon that veers towards an aubergine darkness against which the orange anthers look exuberant. It has up to four or five very fragrant flowers. Grows in soils from alkaline to mildly acid. One of the last to appear above ground and a late bloomer, perhaps opening at the end of summer.

Group 5b

L. amabile This is one of the easier species in cultivation and one of many that have been involved in the breeding of Asiatic hybrids. Nodding Martagon-shaped flowers of red with black dots are hung from stems 45cm–1m (18in–3ft) tall. Plenty of bulblets, especially from around the less stout stems.

L. callosum Slender but strong stems reach as high as 1–1.2m (3–4ft) and carry perhaps five

or six flowers. These are tightly curled balls that open later than many species. The colour is a rather matt red but brighter orange when open. The shortish flower stalks make the flowerheads somewhat narrow. It is not difficult to grow from seed, though we have not found it a particularly long-lived plant. There is a yellow form, *L. callosum* var. *flaviforum*.

L. cernuum Nodding turk's caps in a lavender-tinged pink with a paler centre where there will be a few small spots. Narrow leaves furnish wiry stems reaching 45–75cm (18–30in) high. A dainty plant with a few flowers to each stem, this species is the important source of the pink colouring in Asiatic hybrids. A lime-tolerant bulb that grows quickly from seed.

L. concolor This dinky little lily is an unusual Asiatic in having flowers that open as wide stars and look frankly upwards. The colour is a similar bright rich orange to that of *L. pumilum*. The erect stems are only 30–40cm (12–16in) high and rarely carry more than three or four of the wide-pointing stars. The bulbs are usually about the size of marbles. It is a sturdy and pleasing plant that grows quickly from seed, which is well worth sowing as it may be short-lived.

L. fargesii A slender plant, rather similar to *L. callosum* but of no particular horticultural merit. Nodding greenish-white flowers with dark lilac spots, often single but possibly two to six on stems 60cm (2ft) tall. Petals much reflexed from the short expanded throats. Thin, scattered leaves.

L. pumilum Long grown as *L. tenuifolium*, this jolly little plant has small bulbs not much bigger than marbles, formed of a few tightly compacted scales. It has erect stems 30–60cm (1–2ft) high, though exceptionally almost double this, clasped by narrow, grassy leaves. Depend-ing on the strength of the bulb, you can rejoice in up to 20 rounded balls of diligently polished vermilion. One can almost guarantee flowers from even very small bulbs. It is a hardy little plant and will persist for a few seasons if not allowed to seed itself to death. Obviously this is Nature's way of perpetuating the species found in Siberia, across north-eastern parts of Russia and into northern China.

Group 5c
L. amoenum Nearly a *Nomocharis*. Little bulbs produce stems up to 30cm (12in) high with one to three pendent cups of mauve-pink. Rarely grown in gardens.

L. bakerianum On that difficult border of the genus elbowing towards the *Nomocharis* and *Fritillaria* genera. An awkward, rarely grown, stoloniferous-stemmed bulb from upper Burma and Western China, growing to only 30–75cm (1ft–2ft 6in) high. The nodding, swinging trumpet-bells are ivory-white, suffused with green on the outside and inside spotted mahogany.

L. exanthum Only some 20cm (8in) high and like a fritillary. A single yellow or lime-coloured bell is hung out. Enthusiasts are trying this in cultivation but it is unlikely to be easy. In nature it grows in dry rhododendron moorland.

L. henricii Another with leanings toward the *Nomocharis*. A rare kind that if grown will do better in cool acid soils which do not get dry in the growing period but are not subject to stagnant water. Wide bells of long pointed petals brought a little upwards from the completely pendulous; pale pink or a light rosy purple. 60–90cm (2–3ft) tall.

L. nanum Of all tiny lilies from the highlands of Upper Burma, Western China, Nepal, Sikkim and similar areas, *L. nanum* is the most often found in cultivation. The other species will challenge the most expert grower and are never likely to be widely grown or readily available garden plants, but *L. nanum* is a favourite with alpine enthusiasts. Stems 15cm (6in) tall have several grassy leaves and a single nodding, open, pointed flower of shining chocolate-flavoured maroon. The colour varies; there are mauve and pink forms, and *L. nanum* var. *flavidum* has soft yellow nodding blooms. Needs a gritty, well-drained soil.

L. paradoxum One of the rarest species, found only in small numbers growing in screes in two passes of south-east Tibet. At present it is not in cultivation. It is as close to the *Nomocharis* genus as a lily can get without losing its papers. It stands 20–45cm (8–18in) tall, with two to four whorls of foliage and one or two scattered leaves below. Nodding flowers are like a snake's-head fritillary in form – with no recurving of the petals. The colour is a dark red with sombre purple admixture especially on the outside; rich mahogany is a good description.

L. primulinum This is akin to *L. nepalense* but taller at 1–1.8m (3–6ft), and so far apparently less amenable to cultivation. It has the same thick-textured flowers, usually yellowish green but generously overpainted with dark maroon in the centre. Variable in height, flower size and colouring; there are even forms with none of the central purple that is normally considered the hallmark of the species. Leaves can measure up to 12cm (5in) long and 2.5cm (1in) wide. Petals of the larger forms may be 10–13cm (4–5in) long if stretched flat but their habit is to recurve strongly.

L. semperviviodeum A tiny plant similar to *L. amoenum*. One or two hanging bells of white but spotted crimson and hung from stems only 15cm (6in) high.

L. sherriffiae A rarity that could easily be mistaken for a fritillary. Stems 30–60cm (1–2ft) tall have one or two hanging bells with fritillary colours and markings: dark brown and purple outside, chequered lime-yellow inside.

L. soulieli Discovered in 1898 and not grown successfully in cultivation since. Though seed has been raised on occasions, the young plants tend to die away. It was first described as a fritillary, a plant standing 20–45cm (8–18in) high, with deep crimson-purple nodding flowers. These are fragrant and normally solitary but twins can occur. Petals measure 3cm (1in).

OTHER TRUMPET SPECIES (Group 6)

Group 6a
L. sargentiae Glistening white trumpets opening after *L. regale*.

Rare, especially in cultivation, and difficult to maintain in the garden. Buds usually purpled, but some more green than purple; flowers sometimes with a whispered pink suggestion as a shadow from the outside pigment. This lily produces bulbils in the leaf axils.

L. sulphureum Another late trumpet, a rarity in cultivation, with large, pale yellow flowers. Prone to virus attack.

Group 6b
L. brownii Botanically *L. brownii* is classified with the Oriental group of species, but as far as the gardener is concerned it is another white Trumpet. It is listed above under its botanical relatives.

L. formosanum From Taiwan (formerly known as Formosa), this is a variable species. Plants close to the sea-line are relatively tall and have been measured up to 1.8m (6ft) high, but as the species makes its way up the hill slopes it shrinks until it is diminished to an elfin size, perhaps only 15cm (6in) tall. At whatever stature, the flowers are of the same form, very narrow in the throat but widely expanded at the mouth. Buds are usually dark purple-maroon, but the open blooms are white with golden throats, though often you can detect a shadow of the outer colouring as if looking through fine bone china. The dwarf forms, named *L. formosanum* var. *pricei*, are the ones most often seen in cultivation. There is something of the clown about the wiry stems, narrow foliage and quite surprisingly large trumpet heads, one to a stem. I have had bulbs performing outside with no attention for several years,

blooming not very many weeks after *L. regale*.

L. neilgherrense An interesting species in that it is found in the hills of southern India, though rarely, and is the closest any lily gets to the equator. In most areas it would be a greenhouse plant with large white trumpets with lemon-yellow throats. All-yellow forms have been noted.

L. philippinense Another of the island Trumpets. White trumpet flowers, sometimes flushed purple in bud and greenish at the base inside. Standing 30cm–1m (1–3ft) tall.

L. wallichianum A very late-flowering kind, not too tall, that makes an useful plant to grow in a pot. Smallish bulbs come into growth late and under unheated glass will often wait until autumn before coming into full flower. It has very proper, finely textured white trumpets with chaste narrow bases that give way to wide mouths and can look very charming. A species found in the Himalayas and not difficult under glass, where it will increase quickly.

THE DAURICUM GROUP (Group 7)

L. dauricum, L. maculatum, L. wilsonii

Characteristics: germination above-ground immediate, scattered leaves with leaf stalks, jointed scales, papillose petals, nectary with hairs, erect flowers, erect white bulbs, stoloniferous stems with roots

L. dauricum This is the name of a species or a form of *L. maculatum* that by the rules of nomenclature precedence should correctly be called *L. pennsylvanicum* – a confusing name for a Japanese plant. The usual flowers are upward-facing, wide bowls with the concave petals showing no reflexing; the tips may stretch out more widely in forms such as the diminutive *L. maculatum dauricum* var. *alpinum*. What is grown in Europe as the typical plant is a vigorous one that grows rapidly from seed. It blooms early in the season, bearing large flowers of rich tangerine-orange and some gold but well speckled overall. It displays notable air gaps in the centre of the flowers where the petals narrow towards the stem.

L. maculatum This name appears more frequently as *L. × maculatum* in lily literature and covers a collection of hybrid lilies originally derived from Japanese species. It has now been rehabilitated as a specific name for a species found quite widely in Japan with upward-facing blooms with petals that narrow towards the stem. Petal tips can reflex. The colours are a mix of orange and tangerine, heavily freckled with dark maroon.

L. wilsonii This may be no more than a late-flowering form of *L. maculatum* but the flowers are paler, often apricot coloured, and up to 15cm (6in) wide. The colour is variable, *L. wilsonii* var. *flavum* being used as the name for buttercup-yellow or sulphur-coloured forms, these being spotted maroon and with the petal centres suffused deeper gold or tangerine.

classification of hybrid lilies

The large number of lily hybrids has been classified to make them more manageable. We follow that recommended by the Royal Horticultural Society, which broadly mirrors the species classification.

Division I
Hybrids derived from such species or hybrid groups as *L. lancifolium, L. cernuum, L. davidii, L. leichtlinii, L. × maculatum, L. × hollandicum, L. amabile, L. pumilum, L. concolor, L. bulbiferum*
(a) with upright flowers
(b) with outward-facing flowers
(c) with pendent flowers

Division II
Hybrids of the Martagon type of which one parent has been a form of *L. martagon* or *L. hansonii*

Division III
Hybrids derived from *L. candidum, L. chalcedonicum* and related European species (but excluding *L. martagon*)

Division IV
Hybrids of North American species

Division V
Hybrids derived from *L. longiflorum* and *L. formosanum* without any admixture

Division VI
Hybrid Trumpet lilies and Aurelian hybrids derived from Asiatic species including *L. henryi* but excluding those derived from *L. auratum, L. speciosum, L. japonicum* and *L. rubellum*
(a) with trumpet-shaped flowers
(b) with bowl-shaped and outward-facing flowers
(c) with flat flowers
(d) with distinctly recurved flowers

Division VII
Hybrids of Far Eastern species such as *L. auratum, L. speciosum, L. japonicum* and *L. rubellum*, including any of their hybrids with *L. henryi*
(a) with trumpet-shaped flowers
(b) with bowl-shaped flowers
(c) with flat flowers
(d) with recurved flowers

Division VIII
All hybrids not found in any other Division

false lilies
Many other plants produce flowers that resemble lilies in some way and their common name alludes to this. The most common are listed below, with their botanical names, to help prevent confusion.

Common name	Genus/species	Common name	Genus/species	Common name	Genus/species
African corn lily	*Ixia*	Giant lily	*Cardiocrinum*	St Bruno's lily	*Paradisea liliastrum*
African lily	*Agapanthus*	Glory lily	*Gloriosa*	Scarborough lily	*Cyrtanthus elatus* (*Vallota speciosa*)
Arum lily	*Zantedeschia*	Guernsey lily	*Nerine sarniensis*	Snake's head lily	*Fritillaria meleagris*
Belladonna lily	*Amaryllis belladonna*	Kaffir lily	*Schizostylis*	Toad lily	*Tricyrtis*
Bethlehem lily	*Eucharis amazonica*	Lent Lily	*Narcissus pseudonarcissus*	Torch lily	*Kniphofia*
Bluebead lily	*Clintonia borealis*	Lily-of-the-valley	*Convallaria*	Trout lily	*Erythronium*
Bugle lily	*Watsonia*	Lily pink	*Aphyllanthes*	Voodoo lily	*Sauromatum venosum*
Canna Lily	*Canna*	Lily thorn	*Catesbaea*	Water lily	*Nuphar* + *Nymphaea*
Day lily	*Hemerocallis*	Peruvian lily	*Alstroemeria*	Wood lily	*Trillium*
Eucharis lily	*Eucharis*	Plantain lily	*Hosta*		
Foxtail lily	*Eremurus*	St Bernard's lily	*Anthericum liliago*		

further information

Sources of seeds

CHILTERN SEEDS, Bortree Stile, Ulverston, Cumbria LA12 7PB, ENGLAND, UK *Seeds of a wide range of species and some hybrid strains*

RHS LILY GROUP (see page 157) *Seed list*

ALPINE GARDEN SOCIETY AGS Centre, Avonbank, Pershore, Worcestershire, WR10 3JP, UK tel 01386 554790 email ags@alpinegardensociety.org *seed list*

NORTH AMERICAN LILY SOCIETY (see page 157) *Seed list*

Sources of bulbs

Europe
BLOMS BULBS Primrose Nurseries, Melchbourne, Beds MK44 1ZZ, England, UK tel 01234 709099 fax 01234 709799 email chrisblom@blomsbulbs.com website www.blomsbulbs.com *Selection of species and cultivars*

CELEBRATIONS NURSERY Tony Parks, 19 Sycamore Centre, Rotherham, S. Yorks S65 1EN, England, UK tel 01709 76980 *Wide selection, many Orientals*

PAUL CHRISTIAN PO Box 468, Wrexham LL13 9XR, Wales, UK tel 01978 366399 fax 01978 266466 email paul@rareplants. co.uk website http://rareplants. co.uk *Species only, some rare*

P. DE JAGER AND SONS LTD Staplehurst Road, Marden, Kent TN12 9BP, England, UK tel 01622 831235 fax 01622

832416 email PdeJag@aol.com website www.dejagerflower bulbs.co.uk *Species and cultivars*

WILFORD BULB CO. LTD 69/71 Main Street, East Leake, Leics LE12 6PF, England, UK tel/fax 01509 852905 (Tony Cross) *Species and cultivars, strong in LAs*

Canada
AMBROSIA GARDENS PO Box 1135, Vernon, BC, VIT, 6N4, Canada tel/fax (250)-766-1394 email ambrosia@silk.net website http://www.silk.net/personal/ ambrosia/index.htm

BRECK'S Port Burwell, ON NOJ 1TO, Canada tel (800)-644-5505 website http://www.brecks.com

FOX LILY RANCH RR#2, Millet, AB, TOC 1ZO, Canada tel/fax (403)-387-4382 *Hybridizer, Asiatics, speciality Martagons*

GRATRIX GARDEN LILIES PO Box 186, Coldwater, ON, LOK 1EO, Canada tel (705)-835-6794 email gratlily@ beconnex.net website http:// www.beconnex.net/-gratlily

HILLCREST HARMONY FLOWERS Box 24, Churchbridge, SK, SOA OMO, Canada tel (306) 896-2992 email putld@ sk.sympatico.ca website http:// www.pacific-pages.com/putld/ lilics.htm *Supplies only in Canada; includes lilies bred in Saskatchewan*

HOLLANDIA FLOWERS & BULBS PO Box 36, Site 219, RR#2, Carvel, AB, TOE OHO Canada tel (780)-963-8153 email oranje@telusplanet.net

website http://www.parkland ebusiness.com/hollandia/

HORNER LILIES 23505 Valleyview Road, Thorndale, ON, NOM 2PO, Canada tel (519)-461-0492

LISA'S LILY GARDEN PO Box 69, Clavet, SK, SOK OYO, Canada email lisaslilies@aol. com website http://www. lisaslily garden.com

LILIES LILIES PO Box 17, Site 3, RR#1, Rocky Mountain House, AB, T4T 2A1, Canada fax (403)-729-3221 email LiliesLilies@telusplanet.net website http://www.telus planet.net/public/mgshol/ home.html

THE LILY NOOK PO Box 846, Neepawa, MB, ROJ 1HO, Canada tel (204)-476-3225 fax (204)-476-5482 website http://www.lilynook.mb.ca

McFAYDEN SEED CO. LTD 30 9th Street, Suite 200, Brandon, MB, R7A 6N4 Canada tel (204) 725-7300 fax (204) 725-1888

PARKLAND PERENNIALS PO Box 506, Bruderheim, AB, Canada email parkland perennials @canada.com

RIVERSIDE GARDENS 18 Pony Trail, Riverside Estates, SK, S7K 1A2, Canada email rivgardlilies @home.com *Supplies only within Canada*

VALLEY K GREENHOUSES RR#1, Edberg, AB, TOB 1JO, Canada tel (780) 877-2547 fax (780)-877-2540 email gardenho@valleyk.com website http://www.valleyk.com

USA
AMBERGATE GARDENS 8151 Krey Ave, Waconia, MN 55387-9616, USA tel/fax (612)-443-2248 *Species*

ARROWHEAD ALPINES PO Box 857, Fowlerville, MI 48836, USA *Species*

AUTUMN GLADE BOTANICALS 46857 W. Ann Arbor Trail, Plymouth, MI 48170, USA tel (313)-480-4675 fax (313)-459-2604 *Species*

B & D LILIES 284566 Hwy 101S, PO Box 2007, Port Townsend, WA 98368, USA tel (360)-765-4341 fax (360)-765-4074 website http://www. lilybulb.com. *Extensive list, many exclusive*

BARNHAVEN GARDENS 1920 Landing Road, Mt. Vernon, WA 98273, USA tel (360)-466-5805 fax (360)-466-1404

BORBELETA GARDENS INC. 15980 Canby Ave, Faribault, MN 55021, USA tel (507)-334-2807 fax (507)-334-0365 *Some exclusive listings*

THE BULB CRATE 2560 Deerfield Road, Riverwoods, IL 60015, USA tel 847-317-1414 fax 847-317-1417 email abulb@aol.com

CALIFORNIA NURSERY PO Box 515, Oregon House, CA 95962, USA *Species*

DAVID & ROYSTON BULB CO. 550W, 135th Street, Gardena, CA 90248, USA tel (310)-532-2313 fax (310)-532-8845

ELYSIAN FIELDS PO Box 1636, Springfield, MO 22151-0636, USA tel (703)-503-0032

FOGBELT GROWERS 5096 Dows Prairie Road, McKinleyville, CA 95519, USA fax (707)-839-1364 email fogbelt@ humboldt1.com website http://fogbeltgrowers. com/index.html *Oriental hybrids*

THE ENCHANTED LILY GARDEN 12827 164th Ave, NE Redmond, WA 98052, USA tel (206)-883-7318

CASCADE BULB AND SEED PO Box 271, Scott Mills, OR 97375, USA email halinar @open.org website ww.open.org/halinar/ cbs.htm

HARTLE-GILMAN GARDENS RR#4, Box 272, Owatonna, MN 55060, USA tel (507)-451-3191 fax (507)-455-0087 *Asiatics, Martagons, species*

HERONSWOOD NURSERY LTD 7530 NE 288th St., Kingston, WA 983446-9502, USA *Species*

J & P BULBS Minnesota, USA email lilybulbs@webtv.net website http://www. jandpbulbs.com

JACQUES AMAND PO Box 59001, Potomac, MD 20859, USA tel (800)-452-5414 fax (301)-762-2943 *Species*

K. VAN BOURGONDIUN PO Box 1000, Babylon, NY 11702-0598, USA tel (800)-662-9997 website http://www. dutchbulbs.com

THE LILY GARDEN 4902 NE, 147th Ave., Vancouver, WA 98629, USA tel/fax (360)-2663-5588 email thelilygdn@aol.com *Judith Freeman breeder and grower; pioneer embryo culture*

THE LILY PAD
3403 Steamboat Is. Rd NW,
Suite 374, Olympia, WA 98502,
USA tel (360)-866-0291 email
info@lilypsdbulbs.com website
www.lilypadbulbs.com

MAK-LEEK INC.
39100 Ridge Drive, Scio, OR
97374, USA tel (503)-394-4455
fax (503)-394-4444 email
plntblbs@wvi.com

MAPLE LEAF NURSERY
4236 Greenstone Road,
Placerville, CA 95667, USA
Species

MARLBORO BULB INC.
2524 Castle Hayne Road,
Wilmington, NC 28401-3357,
USA tel (910)-762-5609
fax (910)-762-4148

PARK SEED CO.
1 Parkton Ave, Greenwood, SC
29647-0001, USA
tel (800)-845-3369
fax 864-941-4206 website
www.parkseed.com

WAYSIDE GARDENS
Hodges. SC 29695-0001, USA
tel (800)-845-1124
fax (800)-457-9712
Wide selection

New Zealand
DUNHAMPTON LILY FIELDS,
Hoods Rd, RD 1, Mt Somers,
Ashburton, SI, NZ
Asiatics and Orientals

ENCHANTMENT LILIES, 41
Torquay, Abbotsford, Dunedin,
SI, NZ *Some Asiatics*

HUNTINGDON LILIES,
Linwald, Ashburton,
Canterbury, SI, NZ
McLaren's Trumpets

LILIES IN BLOOM, RD2,
Takaka, SI, NZ
tel 64-3-525-8353 email
info@bloom.co.nz website
http:wwww. bloom.co.nz

LILIES INTERNATIONAL LTD
Fairfield Road, Levin, NI, NZ
tel/fax 64-6-368-5819
*Hybridizers, wholesale Asiatics,
Orientals*

LILIES UNLIMITED
88 Ngaroto Road, PO Box 300,
Te Awamutu, NI, NZ
tel 64-7-871-7588

WESTHURST GARDEN
NURSERY, 52 Old West Coast
Road, No. 6 RD, Christchurch,
SI, NZ tel (03)-342-9545
Canterbury Hybrid Trumpets

Australia
THE AUSTRALIAN LILIUM
SOCIETY
PO Box 208, Monbulk,
Victoria 3793, Australia
will provide suppliers

Suppliers of cultures for
tissue and embryo

UK
CHEMPAC
Garden Direct, Geddings
Road, Hoddesdon, Herts EN11
0LR Electromail PO Box 33,
Corby, Northants NN17 9EL,
UK
01992 890550

TETRA
Lambert Court, Chestnut
Avenue, Eastleigh, Hants SO53
3ZQ, UK
02380 620500

THERMOFORCE LTD
Wakefield Road, Cockermouth,
Cumbria CA13 0HS, UK
01900 823231

USA
CAROLINA BIOLOGICAL
SUPPLY CO., 2700 York Road,
Burlington, NC 27215,
USA

GIBCO, 519 Aldo Avenue,
Santa Clara, CA 95050, USA

SIGMA CHEMICAL CO.
PO Box 14508, St Louis, MO
63178, USA

VWR SCIENTIFIC,
PO Box 3551, Seattle,
WA 98124, USA

Lily societies
England
RHS LILY GROUP
Produces annual *Lilies and
Related Plants* plus periodic
newsletters. Arranges visits to
gardens of interest. Many join
group to receive the extensive
co-operative seed list.

USA
N. AMERICAN LILY SOCIETY
Publications, shows, seed

Canada
ALBERTA REGIONAL LILY
SOCIETY
http://www.tigerlily.ca/arls

CANADIAN PRAIRIES
email mlily@sk.sympatico.ca

MANITOBA REGIONAL LILY
SOCIETY
website
http://www.manitobalilies.ca

ONTARIO REGIONAL LILY
SOCIETY email
schieman@hotmail.com

S. SASK. LILY SOCIETY
http://www.ss/s.ca

VICTORIA LILY SOCIETY

Australia
THE AUSTRALIAN LILIUM
SOCIETY
Branches in all main parts

New Zealand
AUCKLAND LILY SOCIETY

NZ LILY SOCIETY
PO Box 1394, Christchurch,
SI, NZ

OTAGO LILY SOCIETY

South Africa
SOUTH AFRICAN LILY
SOCIETY

North American readers and
indeed most enthusiasts will
find interesting information on:
pine.usask.ca/cofa/department
s/hort/hortinfo/misc/ whose
topics include lilies.

Websites
ROYAL HORTICULTURAL
SOCIETY www.rhs.org.uk

RHS ADVISORY SERVICE
tel. 01483 224234
www.rhs.org.uk/science/mn-
advisory-service.asp

RHS LILY GROUP
www.rhslilygroup.org

NORTH AMERICAN LILY
SOCIETY
http://www. lilies.org/

Literature

Fox, Derek, *Growing Lilies*,
Christopher Helm 1985

Jefferson-Brown, Michael, *The
Lily*, David & Charles 1988

Jefferson-Brown, Michael, *The
Gardener's Guide to Growing Lilies*,
David & Charles 1995

Jefferson-Brown, Michael,
Lilies, RHS/Cassell Wisley
Guide 2002

McRae, Edward Austin, *Lilies*,
Timber Press 1998

Synge, P.M., *Lilies*, Batsford 1980

Woodcock, H.B.D. and Stearn,
W. T., *Lilies of the World*, Country
Life 1950

Lily Yearbooks of the North
American Lily Society

Key names

No attempt has been made in
this book to detail all the key
individuals involved in lily
culture, but you are likely to
come across the following:

BILL DOREEN The
mainspring of International
Lilies in New Zealand,
specialists in Oriental lilies.
Introduced Casa Blanca.

JUDITH FREEMAN Runs The
Lily Garden in the USA and
has been responsible for much
scientific and technological
research into lily breeding.

VICKI MATTHEWS The
registrar for the lily genus,
based at the RHS Gardens,
Wisley, England, U.K.
Supplements to the main
register are published to keep
information up to date. There
are still too many lilies that
have not been registered.
Those contemplating naming a
new cultivar can obtain a form
from the registrar.

EDWARD MCRAE After
training at the Royal Botanic
Garden in Edinburgh,
Scotland, joined the Jan de
Graaff team at the Oregon
Bulb Farms. Now a leading
breeder and authority.

PETER SCHENK Director of
breeding and research with
Bischoff Tulleken Lelies BV in
Holland. Has pioneered much
of the huge wave of breeding
and technology.

The details included here are
correct at the time of going to
press, but the publishers take
no responsibility for future
changes in website addresses
or telephone numbers.

index

Author's acknowledgments

Many people should be thanked for their contribution to this book. Jane O' Shea of Quadrille and Susanne Mitchell of the RHS conceived and nurtured the idea of the book and Carole McGlynn was its dedicated midwife and editor. Paul Welti has been responsible for the book's elegant design. Andrew Lawson spent much of one summer season photographing lily species and cultivars as they opened, while Sarah Cuttle took all the practical shots. The majority of flowers were photographed in the author's garden but others in the splendid woodland garden of the successful enthusiast Tim Whiteley, where many species grow better than in their native stations. John Berkeley kindly allowed free access to the gardens at Spetchley Park outside Worcester, England, where *L. martagon* and *L. monadelphum* in particular run riot. Ron Blom of Bloms Bulbs donated bulbs of a large number of cultivars so that they could be grown on for photographing, and Tony Cross and his wife gave glorious cut flowers from their Chelsea Flower Show exhibits to provide important lily portraits. Dr Alan Leslie, the former lily registrar at Wisley, has courteously answered all my queries about parentage and dates of introduction.

Photographic acknowledgments

The publishers thank those who have contributed photographs to this book. All photographs are by Andrew Lawson except those by Sarah Cuttle (pages: 16; 19 top left, top right, top centre; 66; 100; 112; 124; 128–9; 133; 136-7; 142; 143; 146–7; 149 top left, top centre; 151) and Michael Jefferson-Brown (pages: 19 below right; 31 below left; 62; 64; 70–1; 82; 85–6; 92; 97 below left; 110 top left). Those on pages 10 and 11 © Lindley Library, The Royal Horticultural Society.